ork. Walkiewicz infuses this comprehensive critical treatment with an enthusiastic rendering f Barth's postmodernist vision of America, lacing Barth side by side with Joyce, Beckett, Nabokov, Pynchon, and Borges. The result is n exciting new contribution to the understanding of John Barth as a daring inventor in the elds of fantasy, myth, realism, autobiographial narration, and criticism. This critical biograhy is both provocative and accessible, a welome addition to the bookshelf of every reader f contemporary fiction and criticism.

The Author

. P. Walkiewicz teaches literature at Oklama State University. He has written extenvely on twentieth-century writers, including illiam Carlos Williams and Ezra Pound. A ative New Yorker, Walkiewicz lives in Stillater, Oklahoma, with his wife.

John Barth

Twayne's United States Authors Series

Warren French, Editor

Indiana University

TUSAS 505

JOHN BARTH
(1930–   )

John Barth

By E. P. Walkiewicz

Oklahoma State University

Twayne Publishers
A Division of G. K. Hall & Co. • Boston

John Barth

E. P. Walkiewicz

Copyright © 1986 by G. K. Hall & Co.
All Rights Reserved
Published by Twayne Publishers
A Division of G. K. Hall & Co.
70 Lincoln Street
Boston, Massachusetts 02111

Copyediting supervised by Lewis DeSimone
Book production by Elizabeth Todesco
Book design by Barbara Anderson

Typeset in 11 pt. Garamond
by P&M Typesetting, Inc., Waterbury, Connecticut

Printed on permanent/durable acid-free paper
and bound in the United States of America

Library of Congress Cataloging in Publication Data

Walkiewicz, E. P.
    John Barth.

        (Twayne's United States authors series; TUSAS 505)
        Bibliography: p. 161
        Includes index.
        1. Barth, John—Criticism and interpretation.
I. Title. II. Series.
PS3552.A75Z93   1986   813'.54   86-3076
ISBN 0-8057-7461-0

Contents

About the Author

E. P. Walkiewicz was educated at Yale University (B.A.), Columbia University (M.A.), and the University of New Mexico (Ph.D.). He has published articles on the work of such writers as Ezra Pound, James Joyce, William Carlos Williams, and Seamus Heaney. His essays have been included in *William Carlos Williams: Man and Poet*, edited by C. F. Terrell, and in *The American Short Story, 1945–1980: A Critical History*, edited by Gordon Weaver. At present he is an associate professor of English at Oklahoma State University, where he teaches courses in twentieth-century British and American literature.

Preface

This book is intended to serve as an introduction to the fiction of John Barth, a contemporary writer who throughout his career has exhibited great versatility, technical virtuosity, learning, and wit. Because of the introductory nature of this critique and because of the formal complexity, verbal richness, and eclectic content of many of Barth's books, I have to a degree limited myself to an attempt to transmit a fairly general sense of the shape and flavor of the body of work Barth has completed to date. Those readers who are interested in consulting critical commentary that treats specific works more meticulously or addresses specific issues in greater detail are advised to begin with some of the items I have listed in the bibliography, especially the fine assemblage of articles and reviews provided in *Critical Essays on John Barth*, edited by Joseph J. Waldmeir, and Charles B. Harris's *Passionate Virtuosity*, a reading I regret I myself did not gain access to until I had nearly completed the draft of my own. Although I have employed both excerpts and my own prose in an effort to indicate the depth of Barth's humor and the intricate and engaging linguistic play that characterizes his style, there is, of course, no substitute for the original, and I trust that any reader whose appetite has been whetted by the sampling I have offered will turn or return to the primary texts themselves.

Unlike previous books on Barth, this one endeavors to present an evolving and multistranded argument that takes into account all eight major volumes he has produced so far. In developing that argument, I have proceeded for the most part chronologically, taking up Barth's works in the order in which they were written, initiating my discussion of each by concentrating on form, technique, and language, and then moving rather linearly through each tale. At all times, I have essayed to keep both eyes focused on the fiction while planting one foot in the critical past and the other in the poststructuralist present. Whether or not I have successfully accomplished this acrobatic feat, I do believe that I have managed to avoid stumbling over jargon. In any case, even though the individual chapters of this study may be taken as standing on their own, because it reflects the interconnectedness of the individual members of Barth's corpus, the reader will probably find his experience more rewarding if he starts at the beginning and follows through to the end.

Where I have deemed it useful and appropriate, I have often included comments gleaned from Barth's nonfiction prose or from published interviews with him. In all instances, I have employed such statements with the attitude that they constitute individual parts of the contrapuntal composition that is Barth's oeuvre and are not to be considered as representing definitive expressions of authorial intention. Similarly, where I have had recourse to make use of generic labels such as "Menippean satire," I have done so in order to provide the reader with an easy entrée or to create a framework for discussion rather than to suggest that Barth's fiction can be restrictively categorized.

Finally, this study is built upon the foundation laid by the numerous critics who have gone before me and who, by writing wisely and well, have made my task both simpler and more difficult. Wherever I have closely pursued their lines of reasoning or echoed their phrasing I have furnished full citations. Otherwise, I hope this comprehensive declaration of my debt will serve in place of more formal acknowledgment. In addition, I would like to express my appreciation to K. D. Reese for assiduously assisting with the preparation of the manuscript, to Michael Wilson for laboring on the bibliography, to Warren French for manifesting forbearance and offering guidance and support, and to John Barth himself for graciously responding to my inquiries. Above all, I must thank my wife, Sally, who not only aided me at every stage of this project but also helped me to regain my bearings whenever I began to lose my way in the funhouse. If, as he has suggested, Mr. Barth has a specific person in mind when he writes, so do I.

E. P. Walkiewicz

Oklahoma State University

Chronology

1930   John Simmons Barth born in Cambridge, Maryland, 27 May, to John Jacob and Georgia (Simmons) Barth.

1947   Graduates from high school; attends the Juilliard School of Music for a short time; enrolls in the fall at Johns Hopkins University as a scholarship student tentatively majoring in journalism.

1949   Inspired by a Spanish professor, Pedro Salinas, becomes interested in writing and teaching.

1950   Marries Harriette Anne Strickland, 11 January. Publishes two stories in student literary magazines and "Lilith and the Lion" in the *Hopkins Review*.

1951   Receives A.B. in creative writing. Daughter Christine born, 31 July. Enters graduate writing program at Hopkins.

1952   Completes "Shirt of Nessus" (master's thesis) and sends it to an agent. Receives M.A. in creative writing. Begins doctoral work. Son John born, 14 October.

1953   Leaves graduate school for financial reasons. Accepts position as instructor in the English Department at Pennsylvania State University. Begins working on "Dorchester Tales" (uncompleted story cycle).

1954   Son Daniel born, 21 January.

1955   Writes *The Floating Opera* in three months and spends six months revising it to suit the publisher. Writes *The End of the Road* in the last three months of the year.

1956   *The Floating Opera* nominated for National Book Award.

1957   Becomes assistant professor of English at Pennsylvania State.

1958   *The End of the Road*. Receives small grant to return to Maryland to do research for *The Sot-Weed Factor*.

1959   Begins uncompleted novel tentatively entitled "The Seeker" or "The Amateur."

1960   *The Sot-Weed Factor*. Begins *Giles Goat-Boy*. Becomes associate professor of English, Pennsylvania State.

1963   Spends sabbatical leave in Europe, living for a time in Spain.

1965   Becomes professor of English, State University of New York (SUNY) at Buffalo. Receives Brandeis University Creative Arts Award, Rockefeller Foundation grant (1965–66).

1966   *Giles Goat-Boy*. Begins "fiddling with tapes." Receives National Institute of Arts and Letters grant.

1967   "The Literature of Exhaustion" appears in *Atlantic*. Revised editions of *The Floating Opera, The End of the Road*, and *The Sot-Weed Factor*.

1968   *Lost in the Funhouse* nominated for National Book Award.

1969   Marriage ends in divorce. Receives honorary Litt.D., University of Maryland. Begins work on *LETTERS*.

1970   Marries Shelly Rosenberg, 27 December.

1971   Becomes Edward H. Butler Professor of English, SUNY at Buffalo.

1972   *Chimera*.

1973   Receives National Book Award for *Chimera*. Becomes professor of English and creative writing, Johns Hopkins University.

1979   *LETTERS*.

1980   "The Literature of Replenishment" appears in *Atlantic*.

1983   *Sabbatical*.

Chapter One
The Maryland Muse

"Every novelist," John Barth once said, "aspires to be a Dickens or a Mark Twain or a Cervantes, a writer who seems able to produce substantive works and at the same time earn a degree of popular acceptance. Perhaps that was easier to do in earlier centuries. Or, perhaps those authors were so extravagantly gifted that their achievements can't even be approximated."[1] This statement, like many Barth has made about his artistic aspirations, points to the at least potentially contradictory aims and limitations that define his role as author. As a maker of fiction working in the second half of the twentieth century, he is aware that the response of his reader has been conditioned not only by literary traditions but by modern critical theories, is conscious that he will be considered by some to be an heir, whether legitimate or not, not only of Dickens, Twain, and Cervantes, but also of James, Joyce, and Faulkner, Beckett, Borges, and Nabokov. While displaying a commitment to craft and form, he has attempted to keep his audience entertained by spinning out enticing webs of story. A self-professed Platonist who has produced substantial books and pronounced them to be passionately about things, he has also devised characters who doubt the existence of absolutes, has undermined the foundations of his authority, and has toyed with a profound skepticism that calls into question the concept of a unified and continuous self as well as all systems of ethics and philosophy. An old-fashioned connoisseur of words who hopes one day to have contributed to posterity a novel image charged with "mythopoetic voltage,"[2] he has written books that seem to embody attitudes toward language that are consonant with contemporary linguistic and critical theory, has played with the notion of literary exhaustion, and has permitted the felt ultimacy of his times to creep into his fiction.

Although he himself has averred that the "particular work ought always to take primacy over contexts and categories," Barth has been called, among other things, a "fabulator," a "novelist of the absurd," a "cosmic satirist," and a practitioner of "black humor" and "the literature of exhaustion."[3] This proliferation of labels may be ascribed to

the dubious critical practice of grasping for a convenient umbrella under which to place a group of contemporary authors, but it may also
be viewed as the result of a series of honest efforts to describe the
nature of Barth's fiction. For, as one of his protean surrogates puts it,
"No one who sees entire the scope and variety of the world can rest
content with a single form," and all of the eight major works Barth
has published so far are multigeneric, blends of the real and the irreal, mixtures of a variety of tones and levels of diction. Moreover, it
is just as overly reductive to fix Barth's oeuvre in a particular historical context as it is to define the individual Barth fiction in terms of a
single genre, for, if his books exhibit broad affinities with those of
other postmodernists and respond in certain ways to those of the major modernists, they also bear marked similarities to, and develop a
dialogue with, a number of decidedly premodernist authors and texts,
with the Bible, Homer, *The Thousand and One Nights, Don Quixote,*
and *Tristram Shandy,* to name a few.

As Barth recalls, his fascination with the old tales, his desire to
return to the origins of his art, stems from the time when, as "an
illiterate undergraduate," he was employed filing books in the Classics Library at Johns Hopkins: "One was permitted to get lost for
hours in that splendrous labyrinth and intoxicate, engorge oneself
with *story.* Especially I became enamored of the great tale-cycles and
collections: Somadeva's *Ocean of Story* in ten huge volumes, Burton's
Thousand Nights and a Night in twelve, the *Panchatantra,* the *Gesta
Romanorum,* the *Novellino,* and the *Pent-Hept-* and *Decameron.* If anything ever makes a writer out of me, it will be the digestion of that
enormous surreptitious feast of narrative."[4] It was right about then
that he was also introduced to Cervantes and began devouring short
stories by the thousands,[5] setting the pattern for future excursions
into such territories as Western mythology, the eighteenth-century
English novel, and early American literature.

My Maryland

Rather than being truly illuminating, these recollections, like most
of the known details of Barth's biography, serve to confirm what
might be fairly easily extrapolated on the basis of his works alone.
Born on 27 May 1930 in Cambridge, the seat of Dorchester County,
on the Southern-oriented Eastern Shore of Maryland, and raised in the
same town, Barth grew up in an area where American history was a

visible presence and where some of the "British locutions" found in his prose "are still preserved in the speech" of the local populace.[6] For a twenty-year span, Barth taught at academic institutions in other states, serving first as an instructor, assistant professor, and associate professor at Pennsylvania State University from 1953 to 1965, and then as a full professor and Edward H. Butler Professor of English at The State University of New York at Buffalo from 1965 to 1973. Nevertheless, he has throughout his life remained strongly tied to Maryland, at least mentally if not always physically. Except for a brief period of study at the Juilliard School of Music, Barth received all of his higher education at Johns Hopkins, entering the university (1947) "rather by accident" and initially selecting journalism as his under-graduate major "because it sounded easy." Discovering in his junior year that he "had, almost without realizing it, become committed to the idea of literature and of writing serious fiction," he began turning out short stories and, after earning his degree in creative writing, felt confident enough about his vocation to continue on in the master's program.[7] After producing "Shirt of Nessus," an unpublished and rel-atively realistic novel about a Maryland family, and completing the other requirements for his M.A. (1952), he enrolled in the doctoral program at Hopkins, but was forced after a year to find employment elsewhere. In 1973, however, he returned, accepting the position of professor of English and creative writing, a post he has held since.

The Maryland connection is a significant one, for, even though Barth may have earned in some quarters a reputation as an experimen-talist, his fiction shares with the earliest of American novels the foun-dation afforded by a strong sense of place. The border state, the tidewater region, is the local through which he works toward the uni-versal, supplies the topography that serves as model for his landscape of the imagination. In an "occasional piece" he produced for the *Ken-yon Review* as the first in a series of "Landscapes," he has us view his Eastern Shore from the point of view of an old resident of "East Dor-set," a replica of the author's home town that we visit elsewhere in his work. If Captain Claude "seldom goes out anymore," we are told, he "seldom needs to, for the creek there by his yard, though it sepa-rates East Dorset, in a way, from the rest of the world, is the harbor of his mind, as for years it was the harbor of his dredge-boat: from it his memory daily casts her mooring, warps riverwards, reaches down the bay, and runs free to the oceans of the earth and all their com-pass."[8] And this, in a way, is also the case with Barth, for the Eastern

Shore has always provided a harbor for his fancy on its voyages into the past or to other places real and irreal.

Except for *Giles Goat-Boy,* which is set in an imaginary "university" that resembles the Penn State campus as it appeared during his tenure there, in every one of Barth's books Maryland serves as either a point of departure or a final destination. The first manuscript he labored on after "Shirt of Nessus" was an aborted work entitled "Dorchester Tales," a projected series of one hundred stories about the region and its history,[9] while his last book, *Sabbatical,* employs as one of its structuring devices a voyage up the Chesapeake. Even his ostensibly most self-reflexive creation, *Lost in the Funhouse,* includes a cluster of stories that contain realistic descriptions of "East Dorset" and Ocean City, while *Chimera,* arguably one of his most fantastic, ends up metamorphosing into a jumble of letters deposited in a tidewater marsh. Running across "a photograph of an old show boat" which he recalled seeing when he "was about seven," Barth came up with the idea of writing "a philosophical minstrel show,"[10] and allowing his own memory to warp riverwards, produced *The Floating Opera,* a book that is, like *The End of the Road,* moored in twentieth-century Maryland. In contrast, as a result of dredging less personal records of the past, Barth devised the basic premise and discovered a good deal of material for *The Sot-Weed Factor,* a pseudo-eighteenth century novel that takes us back to colonial Dorset and environs. The inspiration this time came from Ebenezer Cooke's original poem of the same name, published in London in 1708, and revised and reissued as part of *The Maryland Muse* in Annapolis in 1731; but, having embraced at least notionally the principle of recurrence, including the recycling of personalities, Barth quite clearly was intrigued by the figure of the poet himself, the last person to lay claim to the title of Laureate of Maryland. *Dorchester Tales* is evidence that the latter-day laureate had become committed early on in his career to attempting to re-create the district's past, and as further preparation for rewriting the story of the colony and its first bard, he "studied a year or so, very carefully, what they call *The Archives of Maryland.*"[11]

Because of Barth's aesthetic stance and epistemology, any particular venue, whether it be modern or colonial Dorchester County, or Homeric Greece, is presented as a partial picture of a protean world seen from a particular point of view, a reflection of a necessarily distorted reflection of things as they may be or might have been. Likewise, as *The Sot-Weed Factor* demonstrates, for him any history of the world or even a small corner of it must be considered to be equally relativistic, just as much dependent on perspective, just as much a product of selection, presumption, and invention. Accordingly, he does not feel constrained to rely solely upon realistic descriptions of setting or orthodox versions of the past, finds nothing inherently more deceptive or dishonest about making the Eastern Shore coextensive with places that exist only in his mind or emending the historical record to suit his own purposes. Although Barth's use of locale may thus be taken as an expression of utter creative freedom and detachment, it often performs a seemingly contradictory function, calls attention to the proposition that out of necessity most people exist in an environment that is real, definite, and concrete, "live in calendar and clock time . . . no matter how that time may be discredited by physicists," and rely "most of the time" on "a very simple, crude, and perhaps old-fashioned understanding of cause and effect."[12] His Maryland, therefore, is not only the place where he directs a philosophical minstrel show that turns all the world into a stage, but also the place where Eben Cooke's flights of fancy are rudely terminated, where Bellerophon's heroic pretensions are deflated as he is brought crashing to earth. It is, in short, truly a tidewater region where various antinomies tug in opposing directions to generate the dramatic tension that motivates his fiction.

The Role of Music

Just as Barth's choice and treatment of sites for his stories have multiple repercussions, so too is the sound of his prose richly resonant, something that is undoubtedly related to another aspect of his background, his lifelong interest and formal training in music. Prior to his exposure to literature in college, he fully intended to become a professional musician, playing the drums and becoming enamored of jazz in high school, and enrolling in Juilliard to study harmony and orchestration. Though he was forced by financial constraints to leave the school and transfer to Hopkins, where he responded to a different calling,[13] he has, in a sense, tried to remain true to both his initial and ultimate vocations by approaching the art of writing as if it were analogous to the art of musical composition.

He has, for instance, indicated that he thinks of his use of sources and conventions as a kind of rescoring, and that he conceives "of the business of plot as a rather exact equivalent of the element of melody."[14] Moreover, not only has he designed structurally complex works by employing the literary counterpart of counterpoint, but he has also suggested that the reader respond to them as he would to a contrapuntal composition. If the reader is unaware of the complexity of the fiction "the first time around," this does not matter very much to Barth, does not cause him to become concerned that his books are overly difficult or decadent, for "when you listen to a very complicated piece of music, you obviously don't hear all those notes the first time through, not in the sense of real cognition." If, however, "you play that fugue or that complicated jazz solo over and over and over again, or check the score, if there is a score, then you can train yourself to hear all the stuff that was there right along, and of course the same thing is true of literature."[15] Finally, to return to where this musical interlude began, Barth has stated that there is a direct correlation between his love of music and his interest in how what he writes sounds to the ear, a concern that led him to attempt to recontact the oral origins of storytelling and to experiment with composing "things, literary pieces, strictly for the oral medium, not to be printed at all."[16] Since Barth's study of harmony and orchestration thus seems to have been to an extent responsible for his efforts to create a literature that forces the reader to recognize the abstract patterns that inform it at the same time that it passes itself off as speech centered in a specific voice, it, like his sense of place, may be considered to be yet another factor that contributed to the generation of apparent paradox in his art.

While there are other kernels of information about Barth the private individual that might serve as grist for the critic's mill—such as the hint he has occasionally dropped that his tales are filled with twins because he himself is one—the reader should be extremely hesitant about taking a biographical approach to the work as a whole, since Barth, throughout most of his oeuvre, purposely blurs the distinction between autobiography and the life story of the "author" who reappears frequently as a figure in his fiction. He has described both *The Sot-Weed Factor* and *Giles Goat-Boy,* for example, as "novels which imitate the form of the novel, by an author who is imitating the role of Author," and both present authorial commentary contained within narrative frames. In later works the pretense is carried even further, the differences between outer and inner, creator and creation made to seem even less certain, so that in *Chimera* a Barth-like character is

permitted to break into one of the stories and in *LETTERS* is given
equal billing with the six other principals.

The Academic Influence

One thing that it may be worthwhile to speculate about, however,
is Barth's long association with academia, a topic on which the writer
himself has spoken in a manner that may strike one as just a trifle
defensive. Asked once, for instance, what he considered to be "the
ideal relationship of the writer, the critic, and the scholar to the campus," he responded by quickly launching a counteroffensive:

This is a tiresome subject. Is it a good thing for our young writers to teach
school or is it a bad thing? It's tiresome because, like so many questions of
that sort, anybody who takes a serious position about it one way or the other,
an indignant position one way or the other, is forgetting how many kinds of
writing there are, and how various are the backgrounds out of which good
art comes. Any kind of life at all, it seems to me, can be shown to have
produced work that you admire. You just can't make any prescriptions about
that. The people who get upset, I think, by the fact that so many of the
writers and poets teach school nowadays, are people from the 30's, when you
were supposed to go around the country and get dusty and sleep in hay-
stacks. You couldn't write Kafka's novels that way. . . . A university-type
might not write *The Naked Lunch,* and I'm glad there are people like Bur-
roughs to take the dope and all so *I* don't have to do it; on the other hand,
I might write *Gargantua and Pantagruel,* and I'd settle for that. [17]

Whether or not we are convinced by Barth's assertion that good art
can come out of almost any background, we may wonder about the
implications of his implicit admission that certain kinds of backgrounds produce certain kinds of art, a proposition to which may be
appended the corollary that immersion in a certain milieu creates certain assumptions about and among one's audience.

When someone demanded to know why he had written *Finnegans
Wake* in the way he did, James Joyce is reported to have answered,
"To keep the critics busy for three hundred years," [18] and it has been
suggested by some that there is a direct relationship between the den-
sity and abstruseness of Ezra Pound's later cantos and his alleged
awareness of the burgeoning critical industry that had begun to as-
similate his poetry. While Barth has declared that "we really don't

need more *Finnegans Wake*s or *Pisan Cantos,* each with its staff of tenured professors to explain it to us,"[19] and has vociferously rejected the notion that any of his more substantial books are difficult, in fact his own fiction has attracted just such a cadre of scholars, and his own considerable reputation has been nurtured more by critical reception than by sales. While it may be true, then, as Barth has averred, that most of his corpus is basically simple, if formally complicated, and ultimately neither difficult not obscure, it is likely that there have been average readers who were deterred by the intricate patterning of his works, by their superficial difficulty, who found *Giles Goat-Boy* more dense than a Dickens novel, *Chimera* or *Lost in the Funhouse* more rife with puzzling allusions than *Huckleberry Finn.* Rabelaisian humor may be accessible to everyone, but one must admit to the possibility that satires on learning can be fully appreciated only by the learned. The moderately astute and prepared may certainly find enough in a single Barth tale to satisfy them, but the individual members of his corpus are so complexly integrated with one another that one sometimes wonders whether he has designed the body of his work with an eye toward Joyce's "ideal reader suffering from an ideal insomnia," that captivated member of the audience who will "devote his whole life to reading" it.[20]

To be fair to Barth, the degree of popular acceptance earned by his books has probably been limited as much by the perception that they are "academic" as by any intrinsic qualities of his fiction, an impression that has been fostered by a certain kind of reading by a certain kind of critic who has treated the author's work as if it were not only responsive to, but primarily and nearly exclusively about, contemporary critical theory, who has apparently presumed that Barth's ultimate aim is to write about writing in order to abstract a postmodern aesthetic. Those who have taken the tack that Barth is fundamentally a theoretician may have been impelled, in part, whether justifiably or not, by the knowledge that he has taught at such hotbeds of hermeneutics as Buffalo and Hopkins. But, whereas this must remain a matter of conjecture, what is undeniably the case is that this kind of approach has almost always taken direction from statements in one or another of the pieces of nonfiction Barth himself has produced.

For someone who claims to believe that an artist's progress can be hampered by too much understanding of "what he's up to" and that "a gifted writer is likely to rise above what he takes to be his aesthetic principles,"[21] Barth over the course of his career has permitted an unusual number of interviewers to question him about those principles, while publishing several essays on specific works of fiction and fiction in general, two of which have been widely viewed as representing manifestoes. The shorter of his formal critical exercises are, for the most part, acts of appreciation in which the author expresses his admiration for a few of his literary forebears and contemporaries, including the various creators of *The Thousand and One Nights,* Tobias Smollett, Vladimir Nabokov, and John Hawkes. Some of the passages in these brief pieces contain oft-cited and telling statements, such as Barth's plea in "Muse, Spare Me" that he be freed "from Social-Historical Responsibility" as well as "from every other kind," "except Artistic," or his prediction in his afterword to *Roderick Random* that trends then current in fiction writing might make possible the genesis of "a post-naturalistic, post-existentialist, post-psychological, post-antinovel novel in which the astonishing, the extravagant ('out-wandering'), the heroical—in sum, the adventurous—will come again and welcomely into its own."[22] The field critics have most frequently turned to, however, in seeking to cull material to support or illustrate their interpretations is Barth's extended essay on Jorge Luis Borges.

"The Literature of Exhaustion"

Printed in the *Atlantic* in 1967 and drawing a good deal of attention, "The Literature of Exhaustion"[23] employs an opening discussion of "the new intermedia arts" as a vehicle for introducing some of the implications of a belief in literary historicism. According to Barth, "pop art, dramatic and musical 'happenings,' the whole range of 'intermedia' or 'mixed-means' art," not only bear "recentest witness to" a "tradition of rebelling against Tradition," but also seem to take for granted "the used-upness of certain forms or exhaustion of certain possibilities." This type of experimentation, Barth feels, "may very possibly suggest something usable in the making or understanding of genuine works of contemporary art," but since he is "of the temper that chooses to 'rebel along traditional lines,' " he is averse to the tendency of his "intermedia colleagues" to "eliminate" both "the traditional audience" and "the most traditional notion of the artist: the Aristotelian conscious agent who achieves with technique and cunning the artistic effect; in other words, one endowed with uncommon talent, who has moreover developed and disciplined that endowment into virtuosity."

Because of this, Barth implies that he is much more attracted by the work of writers such as Borges and Samuel Beckett, "people whose artistic thinking is as hip as any French new-novelist's, but who manage nonetheless to speak eloquently and memorably to our still-human hearts and conditions, as the great artists have always done." Both Beckett and Borges, he argues, have created fiction that "reflects and deals," "technically" as well as "thematically," with the "*felt* ultimacies" of their age, but Beckett has painted himself into a "convenient corner" where the only perfectly ultimate statement would be his refusal "to create altogether," and Barth, therefore, finds that, of the two, Borges has devised the more interesting strategy for exemplifying and employing ultimacy, exploiting the concept of literary "exhaustion." What he finds particularly intriguing about the Argentine's "comments on imaginary books," his invention of characters who recompose classic texts or create encyclopaedias that "elaborate" in "every aspect" hypothetical worlds, is that they serve as a means by which the artist may paradoxically transcend "what had appeared to be his refutation, in the same way that the mystic who transcends finitude is said to be enabled to live, spiritually and physically, in the finite world."

Proceeding from the premise "that intellectual and literary history has been Baroque," has "pretty well exhausted the possibilities of novelty," Borges, in stories such as "Pierre Menard, Author of the *Quixote,*" turns ultimacy against itself, uses the notion that no one can possibly add "to the sum of 'original' literature" to produce "remarkable and original" works of literature. Imagining labyrinths and libraries that embody "all the possibilities of choice," or contain "every possible book and statement," and exhausting by inference every potential alternative or combination, Borges manages not only to acknowledge the fact that the number of conceivable propositions of philosophy or forms of expression is finite, but frees himself of the obligation to explore every imaginable avenue or permutation and exerts that freedom to complete his "heroic" labors, make the most of his "insight" and "poetic power." Even if the perception that certain literary forms have been "used up" is a historical fact and not just a feeling shared by writers working in an "apocalyptic ambience," this, Barth proposes, should not be viewed as a "cause for alarm," for Borges has demonstrated how an artist may confront "an intellectual dead end" and employ "it against itself to accomplish new human work."

"The Literature of Replenishment"

Thirteen years after "The Literature of Exhaustion" first appeared in print, Barth followed it up with "The Literature of Replenishment,"[24] a companion piece in which he makes the most of hindsight and new insights gained from both reading and writing to reclarify some of the statements made and reconsider some of the issues raised in the earlier essay. Noting that many had misread "The Literature of Exhaustion," and implying that he himself has reinterpreted his intentions, he submits that what it "was really about" was "the effective 'exhaustion' not of language or of literature but of the aesthetic of high modernism." While "a great many people" may have mistakenly assumed that he meant to suggest "that literature, at least fiction, is *kaput,*" in fact he was concerned in 1967 with "the working out, not of the next-best thing after modernism, but of the *best next* thing: what is gropingly now called postmodernist fiction."

Seeking in "The Literature of Replenishment" to outline a program for bringing that "best next thing" into being, Barth first canvasses critical opinion and lists of postmodernists and then offers his own elastic proposal. Pointing out that, contrary to what some artists may want to believe, the history of the first half of the twentieth century, like earlier history, *"did* happen," he asserts that "it is no longer necessary, if it ever was," to repudiate either "the whole modernist enterprise" or what preceded it:

If the modernists, carrying the torch of romanticism, taught us that linearity, rationality, consciousness, cause and effect, naive illusionism, transparent language, innocent anecdote, and middle-class moral conventions are not the whole story, then from the perspective of these closing decades of our century we may appreciate that the contraries of these things are not the whole story either. Disjunction, simultaneity, irrationalism, anti-illusionism, self-reflexiveness, medium-as-message, political olympianism, and a moral pluralism approaching moral entropy—these are not the whole story either.

Thus, a "worthy program for postmodernist fiction," Barth offers, "is the synthesis or transcension of these antitheses, which may be summed up as premodernist and modernist modes of writing," while the worthy postmodernist writer, he hints, is he who can manage to please more than one audience, can remain true to his own "high standards of craftsmanship" yet avoid producing fiction characterized by the "famous relative difficulty of access" that has limited the readership of "James Joyce & Co."

This time around, the heroes of the piece are not Beckett or Borges ("an exemplar," now, of "*dernier cri* modernism"), but Italo Calvino and Gabriel García Márquez. The Italian, we are told, is to be admired for his "beautifully written, enormously appealing space-age fables," "flights" that are grounded in "local, palpable detail" and that have as their themes "love and loss, change and permanence, illusion and reality." "A true postmodernist," Calvino achieves in *Cosmicomics* the kind of synthesis Barth describes by keeping "one foot always in the narrative past" and "one foot in, one might say, the Parisian structuralist present." It is on Márquez, however, that Barth bestows the bulk of his praise, describing *One Hundred Years of Solitude* as "a masterpiece not only artistically admirable but humanly wise, lovable, literally marvelous." Successfully synthesizing "straightforwardness and artifice, realism and magic and myth, political passion and nonpolitical artistry, characterization and caricature, humor and terror," the book not only proves that Barth's "program for postmodernism is achievable" but attests to the fact that its Colombian author is a worthy successor to Cervantes and Borges, an exemplary "master of the storyteller's art."

From Exhaustion to Replenishment

Taken together, the two essays may be viewed as broadly charting the course of Barth's own career, his own movement, whether straightforward or parodic, from formal realism through the formalism of *dernier cri* modernism and the "literature of exhaustion" to a "literature of replenishment" predicated on apparently altered attitudes toward artistry and audience. It is probably safer, however, to consider the relationship of both the essays and this schema to the ontogeny of Barth's corpus as metaphoric rather than strictly exegetic or completely correlative. One reason for counseling such caution is the disorienting fact that Barth's critical statements tend to turn up in his fiction, where, like everything else, they are likely to metamorphose or become the object of satiric wit; another, the demonstrable thesis that, whereas Barth has produced individual books that may be labeled as primarily "premodernist," "modernist," or "postmodernist" according to his own definitions, all of his creations are the product of a "synthesis or transcension" of these "modes of writing" and their associated antitheses.

Indeed, as should be clear to the reader even at this early point, if Barth has earned the high praise he himself has received from some, if he deserves to be called the "best writer of fiction we have at present, and one of the best we have ever had,"[25] it is because he has given form and substance to a body of work that is traditional, contemporary, and trailblazing, consistent and evolutionary, self-affirming and self-questioning, that acknowledges contradictions and contrarieties and enlists them in the service of art and humanity. Courting the muse in Maryland and other border states, he, like Calvino, has always kept one foot in the narrative past and the other in the structuralist or poststructuralist present, one eye focused on the real, the other gazing at the visionary or irreal. While his tales may claim to be only about themselves, or about nothing, they also give the impression that they are about a more universal business, about exploring possible ways of escaping labyrinths and limitations, a few of which paths are enobling and enriching, others, as his first two books attest, debilitating and "deathy."

Chapter Two
To Be or Not to Be

At the end of *The Floating Opera*, Todd Andrews, having failed to commit suicide and having rejected the existence of absolutes, decides that he will probably go on behaving much as before, "as a rabbit shot on the run keeps running in the same direction until death overtakes him."[1] At the conclusion of *The End of the Road*, Jacob Horner, leaving belongings, feeling, and responsibility behind him, steps into a taxi and indicates with one word his condition and destination: "Terminal."[2] The obvious similarity between these expressions of disposition is but one of the many links between Barth's first two published novels.

Barth composed both novels with unusual dispatch in a single year (1955), and later labeled them a "nihilistic comedy" and a "nihilistic tragedy," indicating that he intended them as the first two in "a series of three nihilistic amusing novels."[3] As novels of ideas dominated by the mental attitudes and intellectual ills of their author-protagonists, both books exhibit some of the characteristics of what Northrop Frye in *Anatomy of Criticism* terms Menippean satire or anatomy. Although Barth has implied that it was not until after *The End of the Road* that he gave up trying to write "realistic fiction," the occasional displays of erudition, the philosophical dialogues, narrative discontinuity, and tendency toward caricature in his first two works are all elements that suggest at least as great an affinity with *Gulliver's Travels* and *Tristram Shandy* as with the realistic novels of Howells and James.[4]

Todd Andrews and Jacob Horner are self-conscious narrators who in recording experience inevitably revert to obsessive preoccupation with themselves and with the concept of self. Todd ostensibly writes out of a need to discover a pattern, to come as close as he possibly can to determining the cause of a single human act, his father's seemingly unaccountable suicide in 1930. Jake's narrative is an attempt to create a pattern, to devise a fiction within which he may be capable of human action. Both projects involve the exploration of absolute and relative values and the nature of responsibility in the context of a bizarre love triangle.

The Floating Opera, Todd's account of a day in 1937 when he changed his mind about killing himself, is intended to form a part of his "self-*Inquiry*," a study inextricably bound up with separate "inquiries" into his father's life and death, all of which involve tracing infinite and infinitely bifurcating lines of causality. In his search for causes, for logical sequences of events, Todd must investigate all aspects of his father's life, the books he read, the people he encountered, while also reviewing and assessing his own experiences and behavior. His project is, in a sense, an effort to create a rational analogue to living. Todd suggests several motives for continuing this endless task: the insufficiency of the obvious explanation that his father's financial failure brought about his suicide, the desire to tackle the problem of failed communication, the fact that his research has become an end in itself, a pleasant way of occupying time. The motive that subsumes all the others, however, is the drive "to master the fact with which" he has "to live" (222).

Todd's fixation on his father's death is but an aspect of his obsession with his own mortality. When he first introduces himself to the reader, he states somewhat defensively: "Todd Andrews is my name. You can spell it with one or two *d*'s; I get letters addressed either way. I almost warned you against the single-*d* spelling, for fear you'd say, '*Tod* is German for death: perhaps the name is symbolic.' I myself use two *d*'s, partly in order to avoid that symbolism" (3). A bit later, after telling us he was diagnosed in 1919 as having a "sick heart," he indicates: "This fact—that having begun this sentence, I may not live to write its end; that having poured my drink, I may not live to taste it, or that it may pass a live man's tongue to burn a dead man's belly; that having slumbered, I may never wake, or having waked, may never living sleep—this for thirty-five years has been the condition of my existence, the great fact of my life . . ." (48). If we ignore, for the moment, the possible further implications of the doctor's diagnosis, then Todd's condition is no different from our own. What is, perhaps, unusual is his compulsion not only to avoid confronting the terms of his existence but to "master" them.

What Todd balks at is not simply the death sentence he lives under but all human limitations, the general absurdity of being forced to exist as a creature that can conceive of absolutes and infinite chains of causality yet must die and reproduce like an animal. He recalls for us "two unforgettable demonstrations" of his "animality" (121). The first episode he relates occurred when, hiding at night in a shell hole in the Argonne, he was totally overcome by fear and turned into "a shocked, drooling animal" (62). What was most disturbing to him was his loss of rational control: "There was no cowardice involved; in fact my mind wasn't engaged at all—either I was thinking of something else or, more probably, I was just stupefied. Cowardice involves choice, but fear is independent of choice" (61). The other demonstration actually had taken place a few months earlier, on the occasion of Todd's initial sexual encounter. Coupling with Betty June Gunter in his bedroom he happened to catch their images reflected in the mirror on his dresser: "Betty June's face buried in the pillow, her scrawny little buttocks thrust skywards; me gangly as a whippet and braying like an ass. I exploded with laughter!" (120). Since the physical aspect of the act is to him intrinsically ludicrous, Todd concludes that to ascribe other dimensions to it is to engage in self-deception: "Reader, if you are young and would live on love; if in flights of intercourse you feel that you and your beloved are models for a Phidias—then don't include among the trappings of your love-nest a good plate mirror. For a mirror can reflect only what it sees, and what it sees is funny" (121).

Elsewhere, Todd recalls observing a pair of crabs mating, a process that takes up to fourteen hours, and again ridicules abstractions and absolutes: "Crabbers refer to the male and female thus coupled as one crab, a 'doubler,' just as Plato imagined the human prototype to be male and female joined into one being. . . . I laughed and made a mental note to make a physical note, for my *Inquiry*, of the similarity between the crabbers and Plato, and to remind Jane that there were creatures who took longer than I" (53–54). Todd's comments mock the suggestion in the *Symposium* that there is a kind of intimacy that makes possible the recovery of the ideal, original self. But though Todd can play the cynic well, can flippantly dismiss such things as the concept of love, even reject the notion that there is an essential difference between human love and crab love, he is nonetheless, like the divided "doublers" of Plato's myth, dissatisfied with things as they are. His laughter, intended to convince us of his sophistication and detachment, seems at times a symptom of frustration, and his state but a step removed from hysteria.

As one who lives his life "in the tension between" gestures of cynicism and gestures of faith (50), Todd both doubts that there is meaning to anything and is tempted to look for significance. Walking past a funeral parlor on the day of his proposed suicide, he had noticed a pair of dogs copulating in front of its door. "I smiled and walked on," he tells us. "Nature, coincidence, can be a heavy-handed symbolizer. She seems at times fairly to club one over the head with significances such as this clumsy 'life-in-the-face-of-death' scenario, so obvious that it was embarrassing" (106). Such "scenarios" create a dilemma for him. To follow them, to accept Nature's "ponderous, ready-made" symbols (107), would be to acknowledge that all life, including his own, is determined by natural cyclicality; to reject them, he must assume that what we mistake for process is only random occurrence, that we live in a world determined by the absurd vagaries of chance. His solution is to try to convince himself and us that it is purely a matter of aesthetics, that his "palate is attuned to subtler dishes" (107), to symbols, presumably, of his own devising. To maintain his integrity he walked on, pretending he had not noticed. But he *had* noticed; he *had* been tempted.

In *The End of the Road*, Jacob Horner's eccentric therapist, known only as the Doctor, advises him that to function in the world he must accede to its arbitrariness:

There's no ultimate reason at all why the Cleveland Stadium should seat exactly seventy-seven thousand, seven hundred people, but it happens that it does. There's no reason in the long run why Italy shouldn't be shaped like a sausage instead of a boot, but that doesn't happen to be the case. *The world is everything that is the case,* and what the case is is not a matter of logic. If you don't simply *know* how many people can sit in the Cleveland Municipal Stadium, you have no real reason for choosing one number over another, assuming you can make a choice at all—do you understand? But if you have some Knowledge of the World you may be able to say, "Seventy-seven thousand, seven hundred," just like that. No choice is involved. (81–82)

In an early interview, Barth indicated that there are many, including himself, who find this prescription difficult to follow:

God wasn't too bad a novelist, except he was a Realist. Some of the things he did are right nice. . . . But a certain kind of sensibility can be made very uncomfortable by the recognition of the *arbitrariness* of physical facts and the inability to accept their *finality.* Take France, for example: France is shaped like a tea pot, and Italy is shaped like a boot. Well, okay. But the idea that that's the only way it's ever going to be, that they'll never be shaped like

anything else—that can get to you after a while. Robert Louis Stevenson
could never get used to the fact that people had two ears, funny-looking
things, and eye-balls in their heads; he said it's enough to make you scream.
I agree.[5]

"A mirror can reflect only what it sees, and what it sees is funny,"
but even accepting that, some of us are seduced by Nature and human
nature into desiring something else, into wanting explanations in the
face of arbitrariness, infinite possibility in the face of finality.

Todd claims to be merely amused by the fact that humans mate
like animals, but he himself admits to being disturbed by discovering
firsthand that they also die like them. He is sickened by the essential
similarity between his father's corpse and a chicken his father slaugh-
tered when Todd was a boy: "Dad put the feet in my hand—cold,
hard, dirty, stringy, scaly, dead yellow feet. I was ill then, reader,
and if I think of those feet a minute longer I shall be ill now. But of
this matter one *can* think, if queasily. Is one, then, expected to close
the popping eyes of his father's corpse? Eyes the very veins of which
are burst? Surely the dirt of the planet would cry the reason for it,
the justification that would brook no questioning. I waited" (180).
Confronting the arbitrariness and finality of his father's death, Todd
can still think, but neither logic nor "Knowledge of the World" offers a sufficient basis for future action, and he seems disgusted that
he is able to go on living in the absence of justification.

The image of his father's body pendant from a basement floor joist
is a constant reminder of human limitation and helplessness, contributing to a revulsion for and a revolt against things as they are. Yet,
if *"Tod* is death," then *"Todd* is almost *Tod*—that is, almost death"
(3), and Todd manages to go on functioning by turning death into
"almost death" through gestures of faith and cynicism. His "Inquiry"
is, of course, the most obvious of these. Todd agrees with Hume that
"causation is never more than an inference; and any inference involves
at some point the leap from what we see to what we can't" (214).
That is a leap he is unwilling to make, just as he is unwilling to lay
his "integrity on the altar of the word God" (222). Instead, his purpose is through logic and increasing "Knowledge of the World," to
continue shortening "the gap between fact and opinion" (215), continue postponing the moment in which he must draw the line which
is the limit of this self-defining activity. But, particularly given his
occasional doubts about the sufficiency of logic and knowledge, his

notion that the course of his "Inquiry" is asymptotic, bringing him ever closer to the truth, must itself be the product of either willful self-deception or something very much akin to faith.

Just as he makes use of his "Inquiry" to avoid drawing the likely conclusion that his father's suicide was the consequence not of a rational decision but rather of factors beyond his control, Todd employs another strategy to maintain the illusion that his own life is not purely the product of circumstance. He knows "for certain that all the major changes in" his "life have been the result not of deliberate, creative thinking" but "of pure accidents" (21). In spite of this, he chooses to believe that he has shaped himself by adopting a succession of stances or masks, each of which lasts until it loses "its persuasiveness" (15), each of which is really a rationalization after the fact. If faith is belief not founded on proof, then the "willing suspension of disbelief" that permits him to view the protean self as a creation of conscious design must be considered another of his gestures of faith.

Todd's adoption of the mask of "cosmic cynic" enables him to develop further strategies for assuming control over himself and the world. His demonstration that love does not exist because it cannot be defined is but one part of a program to achieve complete emotional detachment and prevent a recurrence of the kind of helplessness he experienced in the Argonne. He is, for instance, equally capable of defining the law out of existence—"That will-o'-the-wisp, the law: where shall I begin to speak of it? Is the law the legal rules, or their interpretations by judges or by juries? Is it the precedent or the present fact? The norm or the practice?" (82). Taking the position that justice in the absolute sense does not exist, he can be disinterestedly "curious about the things the law can be made to do" (82), can view it as another logical analogue to life which he, as an attorney, may manipulate without being concerned about the consequences. Even though the financial future of his friends Harrison and Jane Mack depended upon its outcome, he considers the incredibly baroque case of the Mack estate to be, like all his cases, an elaborate and amusing game in which he can demonstrate his mastery of logic and pretend to turn death into "almost death" without worrying about the penalty for failure: "What advantage was there in delay, if any? And how could one delay the appeal? The advantage was negative: that is, I was certain of defeat if there was no delay; if there were any, I might very possibly still be defeated, but there would be more time for something to turn up. So, I suppose, a condemned man snatches at a day's reprieve, still hoping for a god on wires to fetch him off, and on the very gibbet, his neck roped, pleads eye-to-sky for the saving oar. Who knows?" (99). Moreover, playing a game in which this case is the world, Todd can assume the role of God, imagine himself completely free of the dictates of chance. Toying with the idea of destroying the letters that would assure the Macks' victory, he decided to resolve the matter by flipping a coin, and then acted contrary to what the coin flip ordained. "Harrison," he notes, "had survived a double chance: that the coin would demand the destruction of the letters and that I would allow myself, a free agent, to be dictated to by a miserable nickel" (212).

Expressing the concept of freedom which constitutes one of his stances, Todd once informed Harrison that we "act as if we could choose, and so we can, in effect. All you have to do to be strong is stop being weak" (97). Thus, he chooses to find a kind of order in the chaos of his room, chooses to believe that any inconsistencies in his behavior are the results of choice. But no matter how assiduously he works at asserting his freedom, control, and detachment, at creating structure and possibilities, as long as he maintains any connections with the world, he cannot, of course, avoid the realization that he is subject to entropy, happenstance, and emotion. The longer Todd works on his "Inquiry," the greater the tendency toward disorder. Not only does he come no closer to the cause of his father's suicide, but he begins to lose control over the structure of the research itself as he seemingly randomly fills a cardboard box and three peach baskets with notes. He may choose to believe that his mastery of logic permits him to play the legal game extremely well and thereby gain control over Harrison's fate, but it was through a purely accidental display of animality, his secretary's breaking wind in his office, that he discovered the key to resolving the matter of the Mack inheritance.

Todd's masks were designed, he tells us, to hide his heart from his mind and his mind from his heart (219), to allow him to cope not only with fear of death but also fear of feeling. Hiding from aspects of his own humanity, he became, like Lemuel Gulliver, a worshipper of reason and a committed misanthrope. Putting on the mask of "saint," for example, he managed to convince himself that he was "in the position of those South American butterflies who, themselves defenseless, mimic outwardly the more numerous species among which they live: appropriately, the so-called 'nauseous' Danaïs, whose bad taste and smell render them relatively safe" (134). But though the masks were intended as protective measures, Todd's narrative describes several instances in which his misanthropy, detachment, and propensity for rationalization brought him instead into intimate contact with death.

Cowering in the Argonne, he was joined in his mudhole by an equally terrified German soldier. After an initial struggle resulting from Todd's inability to reason with him, the two impulsively embraced, immediately reaching what Todd calls "a complete and, to my knowledge, unique understanding" (64). Enjoying for a few hours the most "intense intimacy" he had ever experienced, Todd found himself free from fear and momentarily cured of his disgust at human animality. Given the opportunity to withdraw and think, however, he began in good Cartesian fashion to question and doubt: "How could I be certain that our incredible sympathy did not actually exist only in my imagination, and that he was not all the while smiling to himself, taking me for a lunatic or a homosexual crank, biding his time, resting, smoking, sleeping—until he was good and ready to kill me?" (65–66). Regaining his reason, and his fear, he ended up bayonetting the German in a grisly parody and reversal of procreation: "At last the point slipped up off the bone, from our combined straining—our last correspondence!—and with a tiny gurgling sound, slid into and through his neck, and he began to die" (67).

While Todd claims that he learned something from the experience, such as to "never expect very much" from himself or his "fellow animals" and to avoid characterizing people (67), what he learned merely transformed him from a murderer into a potential victim. Reencountering Betty June, now a prostitute, in a brothel after the war, he casually mentioned that one of her former lovers was killed in the war and, in an equally matter of fact manner, alluded to the, for him, humorous episode of the mirror. Although "she certainly appeared affectionate enough" (131), she responded less matter of factly by attempting to kill him with a broken alcohol bottle.

Writing years later, Todd admits that he "had done to Betty June a thing warranting murder at her hands" (138), but he feels no remorse for his actions, is simply perplexed that he is often not aware of things that are obvious to others, something he finds distressing only when it leads to his "not jumping clear of dangerous animals like poor Betty" (139). The root of this minor problem, as he sees it, is not a lack of empathy or simple common sense, but the fact "that out of any situation" he "can usually interpret a number of possible significances, often conflicting, sometimes contradictory" (139). Viewing the incident purely in terms of the logical possibilities, why should he have assumed that Betty June would not react in a number of different ways, having forgotten the affair in his bedroom, having arrived over the years at a philosophical position similar to his own, or having been molded by circumstances into a compliant creature grateful for his patronage?

Betty June's attack may have forced him to assume a different mask—it was soon after that he became a "saint"—but it failed to cure him of his intellectual illness and "sick heart" and exacerbated his misanthropy. One might think that Todd's brushes with death, his inability to insulate himself from chance and emotion, would have convinced him of the limitations and danger of logic and even, perhaps, of the inutility of the Doctor's concept of "Knowledge of the World." Todd's need to master the fact with which he lives, however, prevents him from abandoning the possibility of control and rational choice. Following Betty June's "inexplicable" and "unpredictable" assault, he merely decided to protect himself by killing himself slowly, withdrawing like Gulliver from experience, convincing himself that his stake in life was minimal, that his interaction with the "nauseous" Danaïs amounted to nothing more than a game. It was while he was in this particular mental state that he began his affair with Jane Mack, entered into a relationship that he attempted to manipulate as dispassionately as he plays with the law.

Todd's account of his involvement with the Macks is, of course, problematic simply because it is his account. At times he characterizes Harrison as a weakling and chameleon who copies his masks and takes on "the intellectual as well as the manneristic color of his surroundings" (21). Elsewhere, he describes him as "by no means either a fool or a weakling" but "a reasonable, generous, affable, alert fellow," and adds that "if this were a rational universe" he would not choose to be himself but "to be very much like" his "friend Harrison Mack" (146). Todd's use of paradoxical statements such as these is a typical example of his toying with the reader, but it also serves to indicate his assumption that the Todd and Harrison who interact with one another are personae, roles assumed as part of a meaningless social game in which denigration and praise, deference and confrontation are all possible strategems for controlling the play. If he and Harrison reflect each other, what each reflects is another mirror.

Todd is convinced that his affair with Jane was initiated by Harrison and that it was carefully planned and anticipated with pleasure, not only as a novelty but also as a means of gaining power over him: "I'm sure they'd worked out every detail, savoring the deed before it was committed, imagining my surprise and pleasure, and my gratitude" (32). Certain that Harrison's "emotions were often at variance with his intelligence" (32) and that, even though Harrison enjoined him not to feel obligated, he really "very much wanted thanking and being obliged to" (31), Todd decided to use these perceptions in preparing a counteroffensive. Feigning more than one kind of innocence, he suggested to Harrison that he was not only grateful, but particularly obligated because he had been a virgin until Jane visited him in the night. Waiting until the Macks were secure in their possession of him, he seized the advantage by revealing his deception, indicated that only a fool could have believed him and that Harrison deserved to feel one "for expecting to hear" the lie and "being pleased when" he "heard it" (40).

Harrison's reaction to the disclosure, his righteous anger at Todd's violation of the commitment implicit in their "arrangement," could be interpreted as either the honest response of an injured friend or the devious ploy of a temporarily disadvantaged opponent. Todd, however, did not trouble himself with making the distinction, for it suited his purpose simply to choose to believe that the Macks, like he, "wanted an act" (40). As long as he could keep convincing himself that he and the Macks were playing the same game, that the chameleonlike Harrison could be viewed as a projection of himself, operating according to rules accessible to his reason, then he could also continue to believe that the Macks' true motives or desires were irrelevant if not nonexistent, that he had mastered the problem of human unpredictability evidenced by Betty June's attack, and that he, in short, had gained control. Assuming he possessed an author's godlike power to form his characters in his own image—the power, for example, to force Harrison to prove his cynicism as a prerequisite for gaining his inheritance—he found this different kind of potency adequate compensation for his growing sexual impotence.

In essaying to make human behavior conform to a fiction of his own devising, Todd has something in common with other of Barth's creations: Joe Morgan, who pressures his wife into living according to his philosophy; the protean Burlingame, who attempts to mold history to the shape of his devious intrigues; Jerome Bray, who discerns in everything the convolutions of his own paranoid brain. Todd's efforts to master even the microcosm defined by the triangle, however, were frustrated when his suspension of disbelief in his own fiction was challenged by chance and by his characters' insubordinate attempts to demonstrate their own free will. Following what proved to be a temporary break with the Macks brought about by his confrontation with Harrison, Todd had produced an outline charting the possible future courses of their relationship. Like all of his experiments in applying logic to human behavior, the outline was invalidated by the world's arbitrariness when he resumed his affair with Jane as a result of two consequences of human animality he could not "reasonably have been expected to predict" (149)—Jane's pregnancy and the death of Harrison's father. Todd found himself capable of accepting this development, perhaps because, as the Macks' solicitor and the presumed father of Jane's child, he discerned in both chance occurrences the means of reasserting his control. What he could not dismiss so easily, however, was the Macks' revelation, on the day of his proposed suicide, of their intent to drop out of the game, permanently terminate the affair, an insult compounded by Jane's suggesting that they, not he, had devised the game to fulfill their own needs. Realizing that his suicide "would be interpreted by the Macks as evidence that their move had crushed" him, Todd found himself gripped by "an entirely unexpected emotion," "was shaken, in fact, by reluctance," and he was able to recover his resolve only by falling back on his skills as a logical contortionist: "What difference did it make to me how they interpreted my death? Nothing, absolutely, made any difference. And, sane again, I was able to see a nice attraction in the idea that, at least partly by my own choosing, that last act would be robbed of its significance, would be interpreted in every way but the way I intended" (208). What he fails to emphasize in his account of the day is that his determination was probably also strengthened by the fact that his plan to destroy himself by blowing up the Floating Opera would, if successfully implemented, have permitted him to take the Macks with him.

The possibility of making the last move in his game with the Macks, however, was but one of the factors compelling Todd to respond to "the attractiveness of desolation, the charm of the abyss" (201). Failing through other gestures of faith and cynicism to alter the arbitrariness and finality of things as they are, he turned to suicide as a final cure for his condition, a final expression of freedom of choice: "There was no mastering the fact with which I lived; but I could master the fact of my living with it by destroying myself, and the result was the same—I was the master. I choked back a snicker" (223). Once made, this decision offered the further benefit of allowing him to close his "Inquiry," since it suggested a conclusion to his supposedly "deductive" exploration of values and actions, a conclusion which, neatly enough, also supported the decision:

   I. *Nothing has intrinsic value.*
  II. *The reasons for which people attribute value to things are always ultimately irrational.*
 III. *There is, therefore, no ultimate "reason" for valuing anything.*
  IV. *Living is action. There's no final reason for action.*
   V. *There's no final reason for living.* (218, 223)

Self-styled rationalist that he is, Todd enjoys thinking that he, unlike Hamlet, finds thought a tonic for restoring "the native hue of resolution."

But he himself admits that the rational basis for his decision was the product, again, of rationalization after the fact, and his account suggests the possibility that, in accordance with his own deductions, his reasons for killing himself may have been in fact irrational. On the night preceding his assault on Adam's Original and Unparalleled Floating Opera, he had experienced emotion for only the fifth time in his life, "learned *despair*, utter despair, a despair beyond wailing" (220) as a result of Jane Mack's off-handed comments about the ugliness of his fingers. Whereas his reason had in the past made him a murderer and a potential victim, it was in the condition created by this emotion (which may or may not have been despair), that he devised his plan to annihilate himself and the world by blowing up the showboat. It is this that represents perhaps the darkest expression of nihilism in Barth's novel—that it was not, or not solely, Todd's intellectual illness, his inhuman rationality, but his "sick heart," his human weakness, which brought him to a state in which he could coldly anticipate the obliteration of his acquaintances and the child who may be his daughter: "Calmly too I heard somewhere the squeal of an overexcited child, too young to be up so late: not impossibly Jeannine. I considered a small body, formed perhaps from my own

and flawless Jane's, black, cracked, smoking. Col. Morton, Bill Butler, old Mr. and Mrs. Bishop—it made no difference, absolutely"
(239).

Since *The Floating Opera* is nihilistic comedy, Todd was saved from
destroying himself and six hundred and ninety-nine of his townspeo-
ple not, as he would like to think, because he changed his mind but
because the unforeseen actions of an outside agent foiled his plan, preserving him and the members of his community. It was rationalization after the fact, once again, that led him to amend the fifth
proposition of his deductions: "V. *There's no final reason for living (or
for suicide)*" (245). Thwarted by chance in another of his efforts to create a scenario for experience, he responded, once more, with a gesture
of cynicism—"The truth is that nothing makes any difference,
including that truth. Hamlet's question is, absolutely, meaningless"—and a gesture of faith—"I considered too whether, in the real
absence of absolutes, values less than absolute mightn't be regarded
as in no way inferior and even lived by" (246–47). It was in this
frame of mind that Todd, acknowledging his inability to escape the
tension in which he lives, to resist the inertia acquired by living, concluded that he "would *in all probability*, though not at all necessarily,
go on behaving much as" he "had thitherto, as a rabbit shot on the
run keeps running in the same direction until death overtakes him"
(246).

That *"in all probability,"* however, must be considered an important
qualification. For Todd did alter his behavior when, approximately
sixteen years following the events it allegedly records, he sat down to
compose *The Floating Opera*, a work, we may presume, significantly
different from all preceding additions to his "Inquiries." Unlike his
gestures of faith and cynicism, all tied to the world through anticipation or rejection and therefore unavoidably shaped by its arbitrariness,
limited by its finality, *The Floating Opera* is a work of fiction that de-
nies our attempts to view it as a focused and accurate reflection of
reality that drifts free of things as they are. Elaborating, in the previously cited interview, upon his dissatisfaction with the world as it
is, Barth noted:

And it seems to me that this emotion, which is a kind of metaphysical emotion, goes almost to the heart of what art is, at least some kinds of art, and
this impulse to imagine alternatives to the world can become a driving impulse for writers. I confess that it is for me. So that really what you want to
do is re-invent philosophy and the rest—make up your own whole history of

the world. Why should it just be Plato and Aristotle? They're nice fellows, but why can't we start over, for variety's sake, and be somebody else instead and have all history go differently?[6]

Motivated by this compulsion Todd, as author, ignores Hamlet's advice to the players "to hold, as 'twere, the mirror up to Nature," inviting us, "for variety's sake," to a "pleasure-dip" in *his* "life and world" (21), producing before our eyes a book that represents itself not as a copy but an original.

Like *Tristram Shandy* and Barth's immediate inspiration, the novels of Machado de Assis,[7] *The Floating Opera* has as one of its main narrative components the story of its own making. Todd's persistent intrusions, faulty memory, intentional self-contradictions, along with his numerous demonstrations of the physical and temporal impossibility of recording fully even the experiences of a single day, not only undermine the reality of this fiction but expose the props supporting the illusion of all realistic fiction. As he confesses while tuning his piano in the first chapter: "It's a floating opera, friend, fraught with curiosities, melodrama, spectacle, instruction, and entertainment, but it floats willy-nilly on the tide of my vagrant prose: you'll catch sight ot it, lose it, spy it again; and it may require the best efforts of your attention and imagination—together with some patience, if you're an average fellow—to keep track of the plot as it sails in and out of view" (7).

Afloat on his prose, Todd's showboat offers a performance that, like the play within *Hamlet*, is presented and named "tropically" (act 3, scene 2). Todd's account reveals the limitations of the language of logical persuasion and rational inquiry. Describing one of the courtroom skirmishes over the disposition of the Mack estate, Todd notes that he was bested because of his opponent's mastery of figurative language: "I believe it was this final metaphor that won Froebel the judgement. . . . Even the judge smiled benignly upon the trope: I could see that it stuck him square in the prejudices, and found a welcome there. . . . How brandish reasonableness against music? Should I hope to tip the scales with puny logic, when Froebel had Parnassus in his pan?" (92–93). The puniness of the language of logic is emphasized again in his record of a dialogue between himself and three and a half year old Jeannine aboard the showboat:

"What's it for, Toddy honey?" she shouted, awed at the *Opera's* size.
"It's a showboat, hon. People go on it and listen to music and watch the actors dance and act funny."

"Why?"

"Why what?" I asked. "Why do the actors act funny or why do the people like to watch them?"

"Why do the people?"

"The people like to go to the show because it makes them laugh. They like to laugh at the actors."

"Why?"

"They like to laugh, because laughing makes them happy. They like being happy, just like you."

"Why?" . . .

"Why do they like being happy? That's the end of the line." (194–95)

Todd's "Inquiries," investigations of causality, efforts to analyze and embody reality in words, would inevitably terminate in such a cul-de-sac, the dead-end formed by an impassable "Why?" *The Floating Opera,* on the other hand, is "calliope music," Todd's attempt to weight his own pan with Parnassus, and opting for the figurative he produces passages as purple as Froebel's best: "I recommend three Maryland beaten biscuits, with water, for your breakfast. They are hard as a haulseiner's conscience and dry as a dredger's tongue, and they sit for hours in your morning stomach like ballast on a tender ship's keel" (52). A sham inquiry into reality, his minstrel show is a verbal composition, an order made solely of words, a gesture made by means of language.

Appropriating the "completely unsubtle" (169) name of the show-boat—"Adam's Original & Unparalleled Floating Opera"—for his title, Todd clearly designates his book as an alternative universe, and his creation of it becomes a performance in vacuo that, like the performance of "the eminent tragedian" T. Wallace Whittaker aboard the barge, follows its course without regard to external circumstances. It is an act that permits him to escape the arbitrariness of personality, as Whittaker does when lost in the role of Hamlet, or as Barth himself does imagining himself Todd Andrews imagining Whittaker playing Hamlet. Moreover, exerting his Adamic power over language and forming rather than tracing patterns, Todd exhibits a degree of control that would have been impossible in his investigations of fact, producing in the chapter entitled "calliope music" a narrative stream that gradually diverges and then reunites in contrast to the infinitely dividing streams of his "Inquiries." The Shandean open-endedness of his fiction, unfinished like all his boats, makes it, like Scheherazade's chain of tales, a kind of permanent "almost-death."

As Todd's final words suggest, in writing the novel he has turned from nihilism toward solipsism: "This clear, I made a note to intercept my note to Jimmy Andrews, stubbed out (after all) my cigar, undressed, went to bed in enormous soothing solitude, and slept fairly well despite the absurd thunderstorm that soon afterwards broke all around" (247). Re-creating himself in a world of his own devising, he may not only circumvent the arbitrariness and finality of physical facts but also dislocate himself from a context in which ethical judgments have significance. Viewed in this light, the book is Todd's case for the defense, an apologia which he, like Humbert Humbert in Nabokov's *Lolita* re-creating his own crimes, produces to convince himself of his "ultimate irresponsibility" (83).

The reader, however, may not leave the novel quite so satisfied with Todd's aesthetic solution to his condition. One of the last passages in *The Floating Opera* describes his discovery of Mister Haecker, an erstwhile optimist converted to cynicism by Todd's rhetoric, lying unconscious with a copy of *Hamlet* and a bottle of pills by his bedside. This image of Haecker in "almost-death," a victim of Todd's, and perhaps Shakespeare's, words, compels us to pause over that "fairly" in the book's final sentence, and serves as yet another link between Barth's "nihilistic comedy" and his "nihilistic tragedy."

Chapter Three
The World Is a Case

Barth is reported to have stated that he "deliberately had" Todd "end up" considering "ethical subjectivism in order that Jacob Horner might undo that position in #2 and carry all non-mystical value-thinking to the end of the road."[1] At this terminus Todd's "almost-death" becomes death, the living death of Horner's passivity, the actual death of Rennie Morgan at the climax of Barth's second novel. Todd's sensitivity to the difficulty of choosing is magnified in Jake's case into a condition he calls "*cosmopsis,* the cosmic view" (74). Like Todd, Jake is acutely aware of the inevitability and infinite complexity of things as they are. He is a Laocoön bound "by the serpents Knowledge and Imagination" (196), immobilized by both the awareness that his situation is totally determined and the capacity for conceiving a "multitude of desirable choices" (3). But rather than attempting to master the fact with which he lives, Jake, "a placid-depressive" (23), responds by retreating into a state of inactivity and nonbeing. Subject to attacks of paralysis, he also frequently finds himself devoid of personality, existing only "in a meaningless metabolistic sense," conscious of that existence only because his "successive and discontinuous selves," given definition by external forces, are "linked to one another by the two unstable threads of body and memory" (36). Whereas Todd admits that his masks conceal a heart and mind, Jake cannot, or will not, acknowledge that there is an identifiable actor assuming the roles he must perform to function even minimally in the world.

If Jake's cosmopsis may be considered as simply a more extreme version of Todd's cosmic cynicism, then the position espoused by Joe Morgan (the character with whom Horner locks horns in philosophical speculation) may be viewed, as Barth suggested, as an elaboration of the relativistic ethics Todd flirts with at the conclusion of *The Floating Opera.* Convinced that "nothing is ultimately defensible" and that the values upon which rational behavior may be based are at best the subjective equivalents of absolutes, "psychological *givens,*" Joe professes to believe that "the most a man can ever do is be right from his point of view; there's no general reason why he should even bother to defend it, much less expect anybody else to accept it, but the only thing he can do is operate by it, because there's nothing else" (46–47).

Moreover, just as Jake and Joe seem to wear two of Todd's masks, they also serve as two of the apexes of a love triangle that appears to be congruent with the one delineated in Todd's tale. Like Harrison, Joe is a party to his own cuckolding, while Jake, like Todd, is a relatively dispassionate "horner." Indeed, Barth has indicated that he employed the triangle not only in *The Floating Opera* and *The End of the Road* but also in *The Sot-Weed Factor* and *Giles Goat-Boy* as a "dramatic device" for developing an extended conflict between male characters who serve as "embodiments of ideas."[2]

Since Jake and Joe may therefore be viewed as fragments of Todd, and since the love triangle is a much more prominent element of Barth's second novel, some have been led to read the book as an extension or mutation of *The Floating Opera* in which Barth, hitting upon a more dramatic mode of presentation, developed Todd's speculation about alternative poses into a kind of Hegelian dialectic, a struggle between nihilism and existentialism, or between two kinds of nihilism, with the Doctor's pragmatism serving as an alternative thesis, antithesis, or possible synthesis. The assumption is that the shift from "nihilistic comedy" to "nihilistic tragedy" is a shift in genre, that, having satirized philosophy and burlesqued its language in *The Floating Opera,* Barth decided to write something closer to a true "novel of ideas." *The End of the Road* is a more realistic novel than its predecessor, the argument goes, because if we are to consider those ideas seriously, we must be convinced of their potential for providing a way of living in the world with all its arbitrariness and finality.

Because this type of approach to the book cannot account either for its overall narrative structure or for certain aspects of tone, plot, and characterization, those who have taken it have almost invariably concluded that the novel is at worst failed, at best flawed. Noting that the "novel of ideology professes to examine the ideas as they exist— in action," David Kerner, for example, proposes that Barth is unable to ask serious questions "about existentialism, nihilism, and pragmatism, because he has made his characters both insane and two dimensional." "To expose the nature of an ideology," he adds, "the novelist

must show its effect on relatively whole human beings, just as a bio-
chemist traces the effect of a virus through the biological systems of
a normal organism."[3] Though much more accepting of the book's
fluctuations in tone, its blending of the realistic and the farcical, David Morrell is also disturbed by what he sees as an unsatisfactory resolution to the conflict of ideas it presents: "Horner's contradictions are
naturally not very pleasing philosophically, however true to the
book's nihilistic theme they may be. One wants some answers to the
problem of how to live in Horner's world, and none are forthcoming."[4]

To expect *The End of the Road* to raise and answer the kinds of questions that Kerner and Morrell frame, however, is a bit like expecting
oranges from an apple tree. Barth himself has emphasized that his
"writing has finally nothing to do with polemics or the propagandiz-
ing of some philosophical position" of his own, and that his early
books are "novels of ideas" only to "a very limited extent," only insofar as "they dramatize alternatives to philosophical positions." His
method, that of the satirist as opposed to the scientist, is not to expose the nature of an ideology, but to expose the nature of all ideologies by "working out positions in order to contradict them."[5]

As Frye points out, "insofar as the satirist has a 'position' of his
own, it is the preference of practice to theory, experience to metaphysics," and he views "philosophical pedantry" as "a form of romanticism or the imposing of oversimplified ideals on experience." This
attitude, Frye adds,

is neither philosophical nor anti-philosophical, but an expression of the hypothetical form of art. Satire on ideas is only the special kind of art that defends
its own creative detachment. The demand for order in thought produces a
supply of intellectual systems: some of these attract and convert artists, but
as an equally great poet could defend any other system equally well, no one
system can contain the arts as they stand. Hence a systematic reasoner, given
the power, would be likely to establish hierarchies in the arts, or censor and
expurgate as Plato wished to do to Homer. Satire on systems of reasoning,
especially on the social effects of such systems, is art's first line of defense
against all such invasions.[6]

Barth's second "satire on ideas," it may be argued, not only carries to
the end of the road all nonmystical value-thinking, including Todd
Andrews's penultimate stance as ethical subjectivist, but also provides
an elaborate defense of his ultimate position as designer of *The Floating Opera*. Moreover, it is the book's dual nature as both an illustra-

tion of the folly, even evil, of attempting to systematize experience, and an expression of art's "creative detachment," that accounts for its philosophically displeasing contradictions, its characterization, tone, and overall conceptual and narrative structure.

In the tradition of *Gulliver's Travels* and *Candide, The End of the Road* generates much of its satiric force through the exposure of the *philosophus gloriosus,* the obsessed thinker whose dogmatism verges on insanity. Like his pedantic predecessors in literature, and like Todd at certain stages, Joe Morgan is enamored of his ability to rationalize and explain his own actions. Craving order, he seeks to define a sphere within which he may act consistently and logically. Believing the value of his marriage to be the subjective equivalent of an absolute, he tries to assume absolute control over the microcosm he has created, playing the role of a jealous Old Testament God by attempting to mold his wife in his own image, testing her faith, punishing her physically and psychologically when she demonstrates human weakness.

That Joe's position is both naive and foolish is suggested by the episode, reminiscent of Todd's bedroom epiphany, in which Jake and Rennie, peering through a window, spy on him in his "natural habitat" (69). Unconsciously parodying his own efforts to regiment both his life and the lives of others, Joe, recently returned from a Boy Scout meeting, first "smartly" executes "military commands," and then proceeds to "cavort about the room" (70). Catching "his own eye" in a mirror, he next becomes entranced not only by his own image but by the sound of his own voice, mugs "antic faces at himself" and babbles baby-talk (70). Finally, seated at the desk where he presumably reads and writes history, he is observed "masturbating and picking his nose at the same time," all the while humming "a sprightly tune in rhythm with his work" (71). Taking off his mask of rationality, Joe Morgan reveals himself to be childish, narcissistic, and onanistic, a Yahoo who can only pretend to be a Houyhnhnm. Like Gulliver and Todd as cynic, he is a grotesque not because he exhibits the selfishness and animality common to his species but because those are the only human attributes he exhibits, because there is no room in his world for humility and compassion, for those qualities that balance out the baser characteristics of humanity.

Whereas Jake's account of this episode seems to be intended to highlight the ludicrousness and the limitations of Joe's philosophical stance and to expose the "authentic" (70) Joe Morgan, the role he describes himself as assuming in his relationship with the Morgans is one that challenges Joe's own faith in the oversimplified ideals he seeks to impose on experience. Following his initial sexual encounter with Rennie, Jake tells us, he had lost enough of his alertness to permit him "to dramatize the situation as part of a romantic contest between symbols":

Joe was The Reason, or Being (I was using Rennie's cosmos); I was The Unreason, or Not-Being; and the two of us were fighting without quarter for possession of Rennie, like God and Satan for the soul of Man. This pretty ontological Manichaeism would certianly stand no close examination, but it had the triple virtue of excusing me from having to assign to Rennie any essence more specific than The Human Personality, further allowing me to fornicate with a Mephistophelean relish, and finally of making it possible for me not to question my motives, since what I was doing was of the essence of my essence. (129)

By choosing to play God, Joe Morgan not only made it possible for Jake to play the seducer, but also for Rennie to reenact the Fall, commit the sin that would destroy his microcosm.

Joe's dogmatism enabled Jake to overcome temporarily his cosmopsis, avoid the dilemma of choice, by defining himself as Joe's opponent. As Satan, he became both void and mirror, draining Joe's intellectual energy by frustrating his efforts to engage and defeat him in verbal battle, nullifying Joe's will by emulating and usurping him. In convincing Rennie of his omnipotence and omniscience and then unknowingly shattering her image of him by displaying his childish self-absorption, Joe may have contributed to his own cuckolding. In any case, his insistence that they confront the fact of her infidelity, view the resolution of her affair with Jake as the factor that would determine the fate of their marriage, significantly augmented the guilt and confusion that led her to die on the Doctor's operating table, the victim of a botched abortion.

"Screwing up the issues" so that their actions were taken "out of the realm of choice" (154), Jake's satanic pose and Rennie's accidental death caused Joe to lose control of not only his microcosm but also himself, reducing him to a man without a defensible and satisfying stance, and, ultimately, at the conclusion of his final phone conversation with Jake, to a man with nothing to say. Joe's defeat, however, certainly cannot be considered tragic in the classical sense, for his egotism is too mean and adolescent to be labeled hubris, his hamartia too obviously an ordinary kind of innocence to arouse pity and terror. Although, being who he is not, Jake is capable of expressing varied, even contradictory, opinions of his opponent, one of them probably comes closest to hitting the mark. Joe, he quotes himself as having told Rennie, is "mainly just a pretty unremarkable guy, more pathetic than tragic, and more amusing than contemptible. Faintly grotesque and in the last analysis not terribly charming or even pleasant. Kind of silly and awfully naïve" (123). As those who find fault with the book correctly point out, and as even Jake recognizes, Joe is no great thinker, not the kind of character through whom Barth can ask serious questions about existentialism, nihilism, and pragmatism as abstractions. But the book never leads us to expect this kind of examination of philosophical systems per se. Its ultimate focus, rather, is upon the social consequences that may result when such systems are adopted by lesser minds, upon Joe's self-defeating and life-negating attempt to will into being a world constructed about his own oversimplified ideals. Speaking of his initial intention to write three nihilistic novels, Barth himself has said: "I had thought I was writing about values and it turned out I was writing about innocence. . . ."[7]

Joe's stature is further diminished, the absurdity of his effort to shape a microcosm further heightened, by our awareness of the Doctor's competing design. Jake's descriptions of the Progress and Advice Room of the Doctor's Remobilization Farm and the Morgans' apartment are remarkably similar. He associates both with a limitation of vision: the Doctor's room, "about as large as an apartment living room" (1), is illuminated artificially; the lighting in the Morgans' living room makes him squint. Both, moreover, are blank and white, like the empty page upon which the artist imposes his pattern. And, just as Joe, in the confines of his home, plays the part of a narcissistic, godlike Pygmalion shaping his Galatea, the Doctor, in the controlled environment of the farm, effects his own portrayal of the Deity. When you are in the Progress and Advice Room, Jake tells us, you are conscious that you "have placed yourself in the Doctor's hands; your wishes are subservient to his, not vice versa; and his advice is given you not to be questioned or even examined (to question is impertinent; to examine, pointless), but to be followed" (3).

Joe, who at one point told Rennie "that he had conjured up the Devil out of his own strength, just as God might do" (68), believed, of course, that by inviting Jake into his microcosm he was initiating a series of events that would follow a script of his own devising. Jake's narrative, however, suggests that the Doctor must share responsibility for authoring the domestic tragedy enacted at Wicomico State Teachers College, a disaster that was just as much a product of his attempts to cure Jake of cosmopsis as of Joe's ludicrous egotism. For it was the Doctor, first ordering Jake to take a position teaching prescriptive grammar, and then altering his prescription to "Mythotherapy," who made it possible for Jake to encounter the Morgans at Wicomico and later to exert his satanic influence upon their lives.

Unlike Joe and Todd, the Doctor is unperturbed by the absence of absolutes, uninterested in the project of seeking a rational or ethical basis for action. According to him, the problem of knowing how to act is easily resolved as long as one is willing to accept two a priori assumptions: "that human existence precedes human essence, if either of the two terms really signifies anything; and that a man is free not only to choose his own essence but to change it at will." The truth or falsity of these "good existential premises" is irrelevant; what matters is that they are "useful" in cases such as Jake's (88), permit the application of Mythotherapy as a treatment for his paralysis.

To function according to this regimen one must behave as if existence were mythmaking, assume, at least conditionally, that we are all "the heroes of our own life stories—we're the ones who conceive the story, and give other people the essences of minor characters. But since no man's life story as a rule is ever one story with a coherent plot, we're always reconceiving just the sort of hero we are, and consequently just the sort of minor roles that other people are supposed to play" (89). Thus, "fiction isn't a lie at all, but a true representation of the distortion that everyone makes of life," and the only things necessary for successful living by "role-assigning" are also the requisites for creating a believable drama: faithfulness to script, consistency in characterization, sufficient imagination to invent roles and scripts that suit the material, the "situation" (89–90). Not only usurping Joe in his household but emulating him in the larger world by mistreating Peggy Rankin in the manner that Joe abused Rennie, Jake demonstrated that at times there can be little functional difference between following the principles of Mythotherapy and acting on the basis of relativistic ethics. What distinguishes the two, rather, is that in the Doctor's universe, or more precisely in this version of it, the standards that govern behavior are couched not in the language of ethics but the language of aesthetics, and the performance itself has no intrinsic worth other than its not insignificant value as a means of avoiding stasis, the immobility nearly indistinguishable from death.

Although his pragmatic programs may be temporarily successful in treating cases such as Jake's the Doctor, no less than Joe, is a type of *philosophus gloriosus* who coerces and dominates his patients and who imposes on experience systems, therapies, which cannot account for everything that is the case. Jake may have been forced to submit to the Doctor's control, but even he views him as "a crank—though perhaps not an ineffective one," "at worst" a "combination of quack and prophet—Father Divine, Sister Kenny, and Bernarr MacFadden combined (all of them quite effective people), with elements of faith healer and armchair Freud thrown in—running a semi-legitimate rest home for senile eccentrics" (86). Moreover, experience has taught him that the Doctor's therapies are adequate only for as long as one can suspend disbelief in a naive and oversimplified version of reality:

The trouble, I suppose, is that the more one learns about a given person, the more difficult it becomes to assign a character to him that will allow one to deal with him effectively in an emotional situation. Mythotherapy, in short, becomes increasingly harder to apply, because one is compelled to recognize the inadequacy of any role one assigns. Existence not only precedes essence: in the case of human beings it rather defies essence. And as soon as one knows a person well enough to hold contradictory opinions about him, Mythotherapy goes out the window, except at times when one is no more than half awake. (128)

It also "goes out the window" when a patient of Jake's ilk, someone "too unstable" and "too unimaginative" to create a consistent role for himself (90), loses the model that has permitted him to construct a functioning persona—in nullifying Joe, Jake reduced himself to a void, to a nonentity "left with a dead instrument in the dark" (197).

Because the *"world is everything that is the case,* and what the case is is not a matter of logic" (81–82), the Doctor's therapies are intended to serve as alternatives to the use of reason, more effective ways of resolving, or circumventing, the dilemma of choice. But if the world resists rational prediction, the recognition of things as they actually are also undermines Mythotherapy. To accrue Knowledge of the World is to become increasingly aware of complexity and contradiction, to realize "the inadequacy of any role," and, ultimately, to be forced to confront once more the problem of choosing.

Not only are the Doctor's prescriptions of dubious utility in the long run, but they are also potentially dangerous and destructive. Divorced from any values, based upon the assumption that any action is preferable to inaction, and failing to provide any meaningful checks on behavior, his programs give almost complete license to individuals who, like Jake, have "no feeling one way or the other" for "humankind in general" and may or may not be concerned about "the plight of some specific people" (128). That the Doctor's pragmatic approach is just as life-negating as Joe's philosophy or Todd's doctrine of masks is suggested by his complicity in the death of both Rennie and her unborn child. Performing the illegal abortion because her threatened suicide would be "anti-therapeutic" (180), he played the part of an agent of death, a performance for which he refused to take credit, quickly fleeing the "mess" (191) he had helped create, covering his tracks in a pragmatic attempt to avoid becoming another victim of the world's arbitrariness and finality.

Recounting his growing consciousness of the limitations of mythotherapeutic play-acting, Jake begins to reassert his innate preference for playing with words:

Articulation! There, by Joe, was *my* absolute, if I could be said to have one. At any rate, it is the only thing I can think of about which I ever had, with any frequency at all, the feeling one usually has for one's absolutes. To turn experience into speech—that is, to classify, to categorize, to conceptualize, to grammarize, to syntactify it—is always a betrayal of experience, a falsification of it; but only so betrayed can it be dealt with at all, and only in so dealing with it did I ever feel a man, alive and kicking. (119)

As Jake is well aware, language also has its limitations:

Things can be signified by common nouns only if one ignores the differences between them; but it is precisely these differences, when deeply felt, that make the nouns inadequate and lead the layman (but not the connoisseur) to believe that he has a paradox on his hands, an ambivalence, when actually it is merely a matter of x's being part horse and part grammar book, and completely neither. Assigning names to things is like assigning roles to people: it is necessarily a distortion, but it is a necessary distortion if one would get on with the plot, and to the connoisseur it's good clean fun.

Rennie loved me, then, and hated me as well! Let us say she x-ed me, and know better than to smile. (141–42)

Naming is dependent on an oversimplification of experience, and, as Barth himself agrees, fiction is always "a kind of true representation of the distortion we all make of life."[8] The process of creating such representations is not, however, in itself life-negating. Dangers arise only if one falls prey to what we might call the "Haecker fallacy," confuses plots with plots, and, reversing the process, attempts systematically to impose a fiction on experience. Fictionalizing his life, Todd Andrews ends up writing a comedy; trying to make the world conform to his oversimplified ideals, Joe Morgan ends up creating a tragedy.

And so, recovering from the Doctor's failed experiment, Jacob Horner, we are to imagine, sits in the upstairs dormitory of the relocated Remobilization Farm engaged in "scriptotherapy," inscribing a pattern of plots within plots: Joe Morgan's plans to create a microcosm, which are subsumed by the Doctor's experimental design, as described by Jacob Horner (in a book by John Barth). The disastrous consequences of his usurpation of Joe the historian, manipulator of people and events, have led him to retreat into his role as grammarian, as a self-conscious master of language who indicates, for instance, that the "life story" he is creating may be reduced to a single metaphor contained "in the latter member of a double predicate nominative expression in the second independent clause of a rather intricate compound sentence" (3). Lest we ignore his implications that the referentiality of his words is a dubious proposition at best, and begin reading his story with the assumption that the book is a realistic fiction in which we may easily suspend our disbelief for the purpose of gaining insight into the characters and judging their actions, the persona who is only in a sense Jacob Horner asserts from the start not only that there are no such things as cohesive personalities to be held accountable but also that the act of writing that story is a performance reenacting other performances.

Like Todd's opening and closing comments, Jake's allusions to the fictitiousness of the text seem intended to block our efforts at ethical valuation. On the other hand, many of the events that he chooses to transmit, in particular Rennie's vividly portrayed death, almost demand that we respond to them as if they were real. This kind of ambivalence, reinforced by the fluctuations in tone which some critics find disturbing, is also embodied in Barth's terms "nihilistic comedy" and "nihilistic tragedy," both of which connote at one and the same time the complete absence of values and the at least implicit standards that must exist if there is to be either a comedic restoration or a tragic fall.

A possible way of coping with such apparent paradoxes in Barth's work is suggested by the presence in *The End of the Road* of the initial proposition of Ludwig Wittgenstein's *Tractatus: "The world is everything that is the case . . ."* (81). The *Tractatus* is an attempt to explore the nature of language, logic, and the world, proceeding from the assumption that language must be linked in some way to reality and built upon a "doctrine of identity of logical form between symbol and symbolized."[9] It would be presumptuous and futile to offer an extended evaluation of Wittgenstein's work here. Suffice it to say that he himself was dissatisfied with the incoherency of the *Tractatus* and later rejected it, and that some commentators view it as a magnificent failure that in the end demonstrates its own limitations.

In quoting Wittgenstein's first proposition—*"The world is everything that is the case"*—and adding "and what the case is is not a matter of logic" (81–82), the Doctor seems to be echoing such estimations. Similarly, Jake's comments on the problems with naming, the ambivalence of language, seem to ridicule Wittgenstein's concern and parody his method. But, though the remarks made by Jake and the Doctor may to a degree reflect Wittgenstein's own assessment of his inquiry, he did not assume, as they seem to, that the failure to demonstrate relationships between logic and world, symbol and symbolized, precludes the existence of values. For, although he states that "it is impossible for there to be propositions of ethics" (*Tractatus*, 6.42) and that it "is clear that ethics cannot be put into words" (*Tractatus*, 6.421), he also asserts that there "are, indeed things that cannot be put into words. They *make themselves manifest.* They are what is mystical" (*Tractatus*, 6.522).[10]

If we are influenced by the disastrous consequences of the Doctor's pragmatism and Jake's nihilism to sense the limitation of *their* positions, if we are disturbed by Todd's substitution of solipsism for his earlier faith in logic, then, in spite of the parody, we may be led to see a kind of analogy between Wittgenstein's project and Barth's own satiric effort to "carry all non-mystical value-thinking to the end of the road." As should be obvious by now, Barth's treatment of Todd's propensity for formulating ethical propositions and Joe's involvement with relativistic ethics demonstrates that he is often committed to exposing "the limits of rationality."[11] To carry all nonmystical value-thinking to the end of the road, however, is not necessarily to deny all values. On the contrary, it may be argued that many of Barth's books, in the manner of much satire, make an appeal to implicit standards and that, through their effect upon the reader, powerfully described events such as Rennie's abortion and Todd's vision of his daughter's death may make manifest values that are not, or cannot adequately be, expressed.

If *The Floating Opera* and *The End of the Road* when taken together work for us in this way, if we accept Barth's definition of limits and find that "through the medium of farce and satire" he has succeeded in evoking "some of the passion and power of the tragic view of life,"[12] then we may also view his nihilistic tragicomedy as a more than adequate defense for the kind of fiction he would continue to write. Suggesting the limitation of all intellectual systems and asserting that all representations are distortions, Barth's first two satires may be taken as "expressions of the hypothetical form of art," liberating him from not only the strictures of the novel of ideas but also the conventions of literary realism, validating that "impulse to imagine alternatives to the world" that he has termed a "metaphysical emotion." Holding open the possibility of values beyond the termini of Todd's solipsism and Jake's nihilism, Barth also provides a defense against the possible charge of empty aestheticism. Physical facts may be arbitrary, but it is no accident that, having developed in his first two books a satire on ideas that takes rationalism and realism to the end of the road, Barth chose in his third to depict the exuberant "cosmophily" of Henry Burlingame and to devise one of the most devious and artful plots imaginable.

Chapter Four

Fancy's Chast Couch, Clio's Stage

Unreliable Narrators

As narrators, both Todd Andrews and Jacob Horner find storytelling, the creation of form and pattern, to be an engaging activity in and of itself. Todd, who shares a surname with one of the creations of the eighteenth-century master craftsman Henry Fielding, employs an extended analogy between fiction-making and boat-building to highlight his own craft. Even though he does not "believe, as many people do, that there is some intrinsic ethical value in doing things properly rather than improperly," and though he doubts that he will ever conclude construction, the mature Todd is a writer-shipwright who builds his boats "carefully, correctly, and slowly" (67–68). Since hammering out his floating opera is a way to keep on running, to postpone arriving at the terminal, it is to his advantage to prolong the process, to devise means of suspending the sentence. Jake, named after the biblical patriarch, one of the world's first usurpers and schemers, stays alive in order to create and keep abreast of plots. Stendahl, he reminds us, "claims to have once postponed suicide simply out of curiosity about the contemporary political situation in France," and it is a similar desire "to see what" will "happen next," he tells us, that has prevented him from ending his own life (108).

Like his characters, Barth also has often expressed his fascination with things well-made, emphasized the role of curiosity in reading and writing. Speaking of his interest in "the old tales," for instance, he has noted:

The element of *story*—just sheer extraordinary, marvelous story—is not what we value James Joyce for, for example, or Hemingway or Faulkner, as a rule. I love those men very much, but it is refreshing, it seems to me, for writers to become interested in yarns—elaborate lies. The *Arabian Nights* may be a better mentor for many than, say, J. D. Salinger. There is a Hindu thing that I've always wanted to go clear through. I believe it's Hindu. It's called *The Ocean of Story,* and I keep seeing it on the shelf in the library. Four feet long. Wouldn't it be wonderful to have written that?[1]

Unlike Todd and Jake, who are, after all, grotesques, Barth seems to believe that there is an intrinsic value to making, that one may find pleasure in "doing difficult things well." It would be hard to imagine, he has stated, "an artist in any of the arts not at least on occasion delighting in arbitrary complexity," what Valéry called "the secret adventures of order," and he has conceded that he himself has experienced this kind of delight in creating several of his works, including *The Sot-Weed Factor.*[2]

The complexity of Barth's first two books is to a large extent a function of the unreliability of his narrators, both of whom are to be presumed as consciously fictionalizing their biographies, both of whom are at times deceptive and manipulative, and one of whom, at least, might be judged by some standards insane. In parodying the conventions of realism, Barth has his narrators provide us with the specifics of time and place—Todd is very careful to give us relevant dates, when he can remember them; Jake fastidiously fixes the moment in which he is composing his account: "I am writing this at 7:55 in the evening of Tuesday, October 4, 1955, upstairs in the dormitory" (3). Once we begin to gain a sense of the characters providing them, such details, of course, become elusive, handholds that pull away as we try to latch on to them. Indeed, as Todd and Jake expose their bias, inconsistency, and fallibility, as it becomes increasingly difficult for us to separate what we are to take as a recollection of fact from what we are to assume is a figment of the imagination, much in both narratives is rendered indeterminate. This kind of blurring of the boundary between irreality and reality is typical of the attitude of satire in general, which requires *both* "wit or humor founded on fantasy or a sense of the grotesque or absurd" and "an object of attack,"[3] while the particular sort of ambiguity Barth creates in his first two books is extremely suitable for a satire on ideas that challenges all attempts, not excluding the reader's, to simplify and systematize experience, consider it ultimately determinate. But, although most of what Todd and Jake tell us is equivocal, and though their narratives are discontinuous, marked by flashbacks, intrusions, and digressions, the plot of neither book is particularly complicated, certainly not in comparison with that of *The Sot-Weed Factor.*

The Sot-Weed Factor:
Shift to Narrative Complexity

In his third opus, Barth chose to shift from narrative ambiguity to narrative complexity, to move from unreliable first-person narration to the use of an often omniscient narrator who relates events in the third person and who sometimes refers to himself as "the Author." As Barth has indicated, in thus reverting to early novelistic conventions he set himself several goals, one seemingly arbitrary—to "make up a plot more complicated than the plot of *Tom Jones* and wrap up all the loose ends without missing one"—another "not entirely arbitrary": to "invoke some of the traditions of the English novel, and see to what account I could turn them, thematic account if you like, in addressing some contemporary concerns."[4] In that one of those thematic concerns is again the satiric exploration of the conflict between innocence and the arbitrariness of experience, *The Sot-Weed Factor* exhibits a definite kinship with the books that preceded it; in that it almost relentlessly calls attention to itself as an adventure in ordering that flaunts the creative detachment of fictional patterns, however, it manifests an even greater affinity with the works which were to follow it.

In response to a question about the role of "social criticism" in his work, Barth once wryly stated that his "argument is with the facts of life, not the conditions of it,"[5] hinting that he considers himself more a chronicler of Gulliverian travels than a maker of modest proposals. Although the ultimate emphasis in *The Floating Opera* and *The End of the Road* is upon basic facts of human existence, a good deal of attention is paid to specific conditions, and the satire is often explicitly topical. The Macks' sexual experimentation, the Doctor's quack therapies, and Joe Morgan's existentialism, for example, all smack of mid-twentieth-century America. In *The Sot-Weed Factor,* however, the kind of innocence satirized is more general, and the book is topical only if the reader perceives an implied correspondence between its themes and "contemporary concerns."

In order to achieve this greater degree of universality in his third book, Barth employed a number of strategies, including "historical imitation," in an effort to liberate the fiction "from all the conventions of realism."[6] In defense of his approach, Barth has pointed out that:

The idea of writing a novel which imitates the form of the Novel, or which imitates some other form of document, is not so decadent as it sounds at first blush. In fact, that's where the genre began—with Cervantes pretending that he's Homete Benengeli, Alonzo Quijano pretending that he's Don Quixote; Fielding parodying Richardson, Richardson imitating letters, and so forth. The novel seems to have its origins in documental imitation, really. So when we get people like Nabokov, writing a novel which is a poem-plus-commentary—in other words imitating another genre—one feels simply that the novel is coming to a full circle.[7]

Like Nabokov's *Pale Fire* here referred to, *The Sot-Weed Factor* is in a sense a "poem-plus-commentary," or, more accurately, a purported account of the genesis of a poem entitled *The Sot-Weed Factor,* published in 1708 by Ebenezer Cooke. But Barth's effort at "documental imitation" is even more ambitious. For, in tracing Eben Cooke's quest to discover his origins and lay claim to the estate he has inherited, he manages to reclaim his own literary inheritance, producing a work that is, among other things, a historical novel and pseudobiography containing elements of the *Künstlerroman* and picaresque. Whereas we may discern vestiges of the conventions of realism in the implied narrative frames of Barth's first two books, *The Sot-Weed Factor* from beginning to end exhibits its fictitiousness, announces that it is an imitation not of life but of other imitations. Often crossing the border into parody, it exposes and celebrates the arbitrariness of patterns and patterning, its intricacies anticipating the artifice of much of Barth's mature work: the extended use of controlling metaphor in *Giles Goat-Boy,* the elaborate puzzles in *Lost in the Funhouse,* the logarithmic form of "Perseid," the acrostic structure of *LETTERS*.

One such example of patterning in *The Sot-Weed Factor* is the language itself, which Barth has called an "imitation" of "eighteenth century prose."[8] With the cleverly contrived sentence which constitutes the book's baroque opening paragraph, Barth immediately draws our attention to the characteristics, the texture of his stylistic imitation:

In the last years of the Seventeenth Century there was to be found among the fops and fools of the London coffeehouses one rangy, gangling flitch called Ebenezer Cooke, more ambitious than talented, and yet more talented than prudent, who, like his friends-in-folly, all of whom were supposed to be educating at Oxford or Cambridge, had found the sound of Mother English more fun to game with than her sense to labor over, and so rather than applying himself to the pains of scholarship, had learned the knack of versifying, and ground out quires of couplets after the fashion of the day, afroth with *Joves* and *Jupiters*, aclang with jarring rhymes, and string-taut with similes stretched to the snapping-point.[9]

Unlike the prose of *The End of the Road* which imitates in its apparent transparency the language of realism, this is prose that makes a show of its opacity and exhibits a degree of structured complexity commensurate with that of the book's plot.

Like the "Aeolus" chapter of *Ulysses,* the opening paragraph of *The Sot-Weed Factor* offers a display of rhetorical figures and ornament characterized not only by such obvious features as alliteration, assonance, rhyme, personification, and epithet, but also by more subtle devices such as anastrophe—"had found the sound of Mother English more fun to game with than her sense to labor over"—and anadiplosis: "more ambitious than talented, and yet more talented than prudent." Language here is as much involved in playful self-reference as it is employed as a means for creating the illusion of mimesis, and we are encouraged to suspend temporarily our efforts to decode the sentence's sense as it forces us to hear its patterns—"found the sound of Mother English"—makes us conscious of its use of tropes and its appearance on the page: "and string-taut with similes stretched to the snapping-point." Working within the arbitrary limits he has adopted and studiously avoiding anachronistic vocabulary, Barth here also repossesses and revitalizes such archaisms as "afroth" and "aclang," just as elsewhere he conjugates anew the verb "to swive."

Pushing language beyond sense and discarding the *mot juste* in favor of the *bon mot,* Barth unleashes the play of words as sounds and toys with the very concept of signification. At one point in the book, for example, two of his female characters engage in a bout of epithet slinging that generates well over two hundred French and English synonyms for "whore." To label may be to define, to stigmatize, but to continue to name ad absurdum is to becloud, to cancel the charge until one is back at the beginning, where nothing has been defined, nothing said: " 'Foul-mouthed harridans!' Ebenezer cried, and fled through the first door he encountered. It led him by a shorter route back to his starting place, where William Smith now sat alone, smoking a pipe by the fire. 'To what evil state hath Malden sunk, to house such a circle of harpies!' " (482). At another point Eben and Burlingame lock wits in a rhyming contest that is interrupted by a comment from their flatulent horse:

> "Is't *mosquito?*" asked Burlingame. "I'll say *incognito.*"
> "Nay," the Laureate smiled, "nor is it *literature.*"
> " 'Twould be bitter-that's-sure," his tutor laughed.
> "Nor *misbehavior.*"
> "Thank the Savior!"
> "Nor *importunacy.*"
> "That were lunacy!"
> "Nor *tiddlywinks.*"
> " 'Twould gain thee little, methinks!" . . . (415)

As Burlingame reminds Eben when he defeats him, "significance" is not a "criterion" for judging this verbal joust, and Eben is unhorsed when his opponent rhymes "month" with "onth," a sound that qualifies as a word only in a limited grammatical sense: " 'To match the *onth* . . .' is what I said; *onth* is the object of *match;* objects of verbs are substantives; substantives are words. Get thee behind yon roan!" (417). Indeed, when they have reached the end of this particular road, there is little in terms of meaning to differentiate their utterances from the nonverbal noise that periodically erupts from that gaseous beast.

But even if afflatus is reduced to a flatus, here, what remains undiminished is the delight of doubling, of toying with words as patterns of sound. On the one hand, this kind of play is, like Jake's comments about *x*-ing, part of Barth's satiric strategy, suggesting the impossibility of constructing an adequate linguistic model of the world. On the other hand, it is also, like Barth's revitalization of archaisms, part of a strategy for avoiding "exhaustion."

Barth is well aware of the possibility that the enterprise called realism, defined by Henry James as the "attempt to render the look of things, the look that conveys their meaning," and based on an implicit faith in a connection between word and world, may lead not to the revelation of essences, the discovery of general truths, but to the kind of futile encyclopedia making practiced by Flaubert's Bouvard and Pécuchet or his own Todd Andrews. In theory, the process James defined is at best teleological, at worst a kind of asymptotic approximation. In practice, however, it, like Todd's "Inquiry," may be sub-

ject to entropy, terminating with the exhaustion of the medium in
clichés and hackneyed conventions.

One tonic for this kind of exhaustion is what Hugh Kenner calls
"the comedy of the Inventory," created when a finite set is circum-
scribed and all of its members enumerated. This strategy, Kenner
proposes, has the advantage of making exhaustiveness a virtue, for it
generates joy by satisfying the reader's desire for completeness.[10] It is
a strategy basic to *Ulysses* and *Finnegans Wake* and one that Barth too
employs when he exhausts the possible synonyms for "whore," when
he has the narrator exhaustively define the four things (no more, no
less) that distinguish Ebenezer Cooke (3–5), or when he provides us
with a complete inventory of the things consumed in a mock-heroic
eating contest between Burlingame's presumed ancestor and the
Ahatchwoop brave Attonce (608–10).

But because Barth believes that the "number of splendid sayable
things" is "doubtless very large, perhaps virtually infinite,"[11] he also
endeavors in *The Sot-Weed Factor* to combat entropy by rejuvenating
language itself, maximizing the possibilities for play. One way of attempting this is to create the illusion of linguistic novelty. This is
what Joyce does when he seems to invent a new language in *Finnegans
Wake,* what Barth does when he reintroduces archaic words and expressions in a twentieth-century novel, where they seem new to us.
Another approach is continuously to undermine the very concept of
signification, diverting attention to what Ezra Pound termed "melo-
poeia" (language charged with musical properties) and "logopoeia"
("the dance of the intellect among words"), to patterns in the prose
that seem free to play themselves out without meaning. To eliminate
repeatedly the criterion of significance in this manner is to allay the
realist's desire to leap the gap that separates the "look of things" from
"their meaning." In place of this, the reader is offered the joy of following a "virtually infinite" number of finite patterns to their actual
or implied ends, offered the illusion that the text is a kind of verbal
perpetual motion machine that counters entropy by continuously generating new possibilities.

Since *The Sot-Weed Factor* is informed by the cyclic patterns of quest
and of the Adamic myth of America, it is not surprising that at times
the design of linguistic play in the book also gives the impression of
cyclicality. Elongating itself by tying in clauses until its grammatical
structure is stretched "string-taut," the first paragraph of the book
finally reaches its "snapping-point," to be followed by four others

which together play another tune, initiate and complete another design. The two servant women deplete one box of synonyms, but with
"harridans" and "harpies" Eben opens another. Although the rhyming
match terminates in "onth," Burlingame "lustily" begins anew:

> *How wondrous a Vocabulary*
> *Is't, that possesseth nary*
> *Noun nor Verb the Rhyme for which'll*
> *Stump the son of* Captain Mitchell!
>
> (417)

Passages such as these seem designed to foster the belief that the text
is characterized everywhere else by a similar cyclic process of replen-
ishment-exhaustion-replenishment, that, at least in this sense, it constitutes a closed system in which the energy of fancy is always
conserved.

A different, but allied, stratagem for replenishing the medium is
Barth's effort to bring fiction "to full circle" by revitalizing many of
the conventions of the early novel. Barth has stated that he "sometimes" thinks of his "writing as a kind of orchestration," that he likes
"to take old literary conventions and re-score them for contemporary
purposes."[12] His use of the term "orchestration" is descriptive of not
only his treatment of elements of the eighteenth-century novel in *The
Sot-Weed Factor,* but also his adaptation of materials, such as historical
documents and Cooke's poem, that were originally composed for
other media. It also emphasizes what should be obvious to any
reader—that the work is carefully and intricately patterned.

Barth's revitalization of some of the elements of eighteenth-century
fiction does double service, for it permits him both to escape the out-
worn conventions of realism and to develop further certain aspects of
his first two satires. The text rather blatantly announces its own fictitiousness, for instance, through such devices as a closing apology to
the reader and garrulous, overly descriptive chapter headings: "The
Laureate is Exposed to Two Assassinations of Character, a Piracy, a
Near-Deflowering, a Near-Mutiny, a Murder, and an Appalling Colloquy Between Captains of the Sea, All Within the Space of a Few
Pages"; "A *Marylandiad* Is Brought to Birth, but Its Deliverer Fares
as Badly as in Any Other Chapter." Numerous variations are played
on one of the most typical thematic concerns of the early novel—the
mystery of identity—energizing the plot through the alternation of

suspense and discovery while also implying that self and world are protean, that, as Burlingame puts it, " 'Tis but a grossness of perception . . . that lets us speak of *Thames* and *Tigris,* or even *France* and *England,* but especially *me* and *thee,* as though what went by those names or others in time past hath some connection with the present object" (137–38). The linear flow of the narrative is diverted and slowed by digressions and regressions, is interrupted by tales embedded within *the* tale, such "pandering to Curiosity at Form's expense" (806), not only fostering the impression of plenitude but also effecting a Shandean burlesque of realism's encyclopedic tendencies.

Nevertheless, it is the book's carefully woven Fieldingesque plot that undoubtedly strikes the reader as the most obvious example of Barth's rescoring of literary conventions. Traced in its broad outlines, the main plot of *The Sot-Weed Factor* is that of a three-part bildungsroman recording the trials and misadventures that constitute Ebenezer Cooke's education in "Life's college" (433). The setting for the initial stage of Eben's quest is England, and the syllabus consists of Burlingame's tutoring, formal and informal studies at Newton and More's Cambridge, and lessons learned from poetasters in London taverns and coffeehouses. Having discovered that "his untamable fancy" (47) precludes his success in trade, and having courted the muse and encountered Love in the person of a strumpet named Joan Toast, Eben believes he has discovered his purpose and decides to create himself by fiat: "What am I? What am I? *Virgin,* sir! *Poet,* sir! I am a virgin and a poet; less than mortal and more; not a man, but Mankind!" (66). Commanded by his father "on Pain of total and entire Disinheritance and Disownment" to "take Ship for Maryland" and assume "Managership of Malden" (75), an estate in "the wild untutored colonies" (76), he attempts to write his own destiny by dubbing himself (with Lord Baltimore's unofficial blessing) Laureate of Maryland and to transform his estate, bend "nature to suit his fancy" (82), by accepting a commission to compose an epic *Marylandiad.*

Eben conceives his passage to be a test of his Innocence and a heroic voyage in fulfillment of "his single mortal destiny" (110), his role as the "midwife and savior" (104) who will deliver an earthly paradise and possess a virgin land. Earlier the whoremonger McEvoy had accused him of total ignorance: "I shall tell ye a thing about yourself, Eben Cooke, and haply ye'll recall it now and again: 'tis not simply love ye know naught of, 'tis the *entire great real world*! Your senses fail ye; your busy fancy plays ye false and fills your head with foolish pic-

tures. Things are not as ye see 'em, friend—the world's a tangled
skein, and all is knottier than ye take it for" (69). Assured, now, that
his innocence is "a badge" of his "strength" and proof of his "calling"
(66), Cooke convinces himself that he is meeting this challenge, setting forth to tilt at experience: "Life! I must fling myself into Life,
escape to't, as Orestes to the temple of Apollo. Action be my sanctu-
ary; Initiative my shield! I shall smite ere I am smitten; clutch Life
by his horns! Patron of poets, thy temple be the Entire Great Real
World, whereto I run with arms a-stretch" (78). But his quest is
more quixotic than heroic, for the state he would preserve is a static
and infertile one, the estate he would claim a figment of his fancy.
The world, moreover, simply refuses to "measure up to his expectations" (231). In part 2, "Going to Malden," it strews unexpected obstacles in his path, subjects him to trials of its own conceiving. His
identity, laureateship, and birthright are all usurped. Abducted by
pirates, he sinks from the heroic to the bestial and begins to emulate
their animalistic behavior. After he is prevented from indulging his
lust by ravishing Joan Toast in the mizzen-rig of the aptly named
brigantine, *Cyprian,* he is forced to acknowledge that the "relief he
felt at the accidental rescue of his essence was, though genuine, not
nearly so profound a sensation as had been his possession in the rig-
ging, which he could not begin to understand" (286). He chooses to
ignore the lesson, however, and, once ashore, tries to demonstrate
that he is still "less than mortal and more." In order to prove to Burlingame that his cherished abstractions do indeed exist "as transcendent entities, noumenal and pure" (419) and that he in his Innocence
can perceive them, Eben purchases the right to administer "Justice"
in a Maryland courtroom, only to discover that in delivering his ver-
dict he has also delivered Malden into another's hands. Although he
might more accurately be described as an innocent Esau in a world of
Jacobs, he continues to assert that, since he is still Adam "Eveless,"
he remains Adam "unfallen" (435). The fault, he finds, lies rather
with Maryland herself, no longer in his eyes a pristine New World
but merely a sordid reflection of the old one. Convinced that this
fallen land of "scoundrels and perverts, hovels and brothels, corrup-
tion and poltroonery" (493) is unworthy of him, he scraps his intentions to compose an epic and writes instead on "virgin paper" (493)
The Sot-Weed Factor, a biting satire intended to "scourge the Province
with the lash of Hudibrastic as a harlot is scourged at the public post,
catalogue her every wickedness, and expose her every trap laid for the

trusting, the unwary, the innocent!" (494). As the second volume draws to a close, he absolves himself of all responsibility to be his brother's keeper, leaving behind the undeniably fallen but "generous and valiant" (505) Joan whom he has been forced to marry to save his skin. In exiling himself from Malden he fulfills through his own actions the prophecy Burlingame had voiced: "Your father, if I know him, will not lose this chance to turn ye out o'the Garden" (434).

In the book's final section, "Malden Earned," Ebenezer sojourns among the Indians, discovers the difficulty of distinguishing between "unsavaged" savages and "Unenglished" Englishmen (691), and learns much about "country matters," including the "Secret of the Sacred Eggplant." Admitting, finally, that he, too, is fallen, and finding that, in truth, there is "no shame so monstrous that one cannot learn to live with it in time" (812), he wins back his estate by marrying himself to the postlapsarian world, consummating his marriage with the poxed Joan Toast. But though the book proper ends in comedic resolution, The Author informs us in his apology that "it cannot be said that the life of any of our characters was markedly blissful; some, to be sure, were rather more serene, but others took more or less turns for the worse, and a few were terminated far before their time" (806). Eben himself contracts his wife's "virtually incurable" malady, sires one diseased child that dies with its mother at birth, spends the remainder of his life with his sister, and succumbs to a disease that afflicts children. *The Sot-Weed Factor* brings him temporary celebrity, but "its net effect" is "precisely the reverse of its author's intention" (818), his later works are not nearly so popular, and even his own heirs have his headstone "graved with the usual piffle" (819), choosing "not to immortalize their sire with" the epitaph he had composed for it:

> *Here moulds a posing, foppish Actor,*
> *Author of* THE SOT-WEED FACTOR,
> *Falsely prais'd. Take Heed, who sees this*
> *Epitaph; look ye to* Jesus!
> *Labour not for Earthly Glory:*
> Fame's *a fickle Slut, and whory.*
> *From thy* Fancy's *chast Couch drive her:*
> *He's a Fool who'll strive to swive her!*
>   (819)

As should be obvious from this summary, Cooke exhibits remarkable persistence in attempting to remain true to his unique "essence," and to impose a single archetypal pattern on experience, even in face of the fact that at best he effects a kind of Hudibrastic near rhyme with the world. His story, however, is interwoven with that of Henry Burlingame, "cosmophilist" (528), who claims to "love no part of the world . . . but the entire parti-colored whole, with all her poles and contradictories" (529). A picaresque master of intrigue and disguise, he plays the "world like a harpsichord" and "manipulates its folk" like a puppeteer (456). The only doctrine he believes in, he says, is that one may "know of naught immutable and sure," for even the assertion of identity constitutes an act "of faith, impossible to verify" (141). All of us "sit upon a blind rock hurtling through a vacuum, racing to the grave," yet it is "our fate to search . . . and do we seek our soul, what we find is a piece of that same black Cosmos whence we sprang and through which we fall: the infinite wind of space . . ." (373). The "pointed order of the world" may live only in the fancy, but if one would "live in the world," he "must dance to some other fellow's tune or call" his "own and try to make the whole world step to't" (357). Immersed in "Heraclitean flux" (357), one "must needs make and seize his soul, and then cleave fast to't, or go babbling in the corner; one must choose his gods and devils on the run, quill his own name upon the universe, and declare, ' 'Tis *I,* and the world stands such-a-way' " (373). Thus, in spite of doubting that any version of the past can be verified, he commits himself to a lifelong quest to uncover traces of his father, and even though his "ties to the cause of Western Civilization" are "slight and qualified," his "mind and interests . . . enormously more complex" (765), he chooses to make history, "to play the game of governments" (180).

Because of Eben's estate and commission, and especially because of Burlingame's curiosity and chosen profession, their tales are tightly bound with the story of Maryland itself, the book's primary and secondary plots inextricably wedded to the (pseudo) history of the plots hatched, stratagems devised, by power brokers who have their own designs for and on the colony. The major characters in this other tale, Baltimore and Coode, are shadowy figures who at times appear to play, and exchange, the parts of devil and demigod, at other times seem to be "simple clotpolls like ourselves, that have been legend'd out of reasonable dimension," and may in reality be "naught but the rumors and tales themselves" (763–64). As principals and principles, they spin out a mercantile history of America that contradicts Eben's vision of an Edenic New World, necessitating his transformation from "factor" to "factor," compelling him to abandon the role of "maker" of epics and adopt the persona of swindled merchant. Furthermore, as the plot thickens, not only do Cooke's heroes, *"fair* Albions *Pride!"* (193), metamorphose into Burlingame's "castaways from Europe" (181), but the grand design of colonialism itself, which claims to plead the case of "Civilization *versus* the Abyss of salvagery" (716), is unraveled or becomes obscured as Englishmen turn native or act like savages and English women, pining "for the black and lawless Pit," unleash the "piece o' the salvage" in all of us and "raise their skirts . . . like the Queen in *The Thousand and One Nights"* (639).

The incredible complexity of the book's plots and the ingenious and unrealistic way in which their multiple strands are tied together at the end suggest that life is indeed "a tangled skein" and "all knottier" than one would "take it for." In effect, Barth employs plot in *The Sot-Weed Factor* to make a formal statement expressing the attitude of satire, affirming the position that no single pattern, even a mythic or cultural one, is adequate to define or contain "the entire great real world," that sufficiency and closure are characteristics not of experience but of art. The metamorphoses of characters and settings that contribute to this statement by indicating the inadequacy of labels may lead us to view the book as resembling not one but several hundred pages "of Ovid" (789), but the metamorphosing of story into story, which is another element of Barth's satiric strategy, is a convention *The Sot-Weed Factor* shares with a different literary classic, Laurence Sterne's own "tale of a cock and a bull" (114).

Relationships to *Tristram Shandy*

In discussing the disruption of "the usual sequence" of "narrative chronology" in *Tristram Shandy,* Ian Watt concludes that "in the last analysis the reasons for Sterne's highly idiosyncratic handling of time is that he wanted to achieve a mode of organization which was controlled by much more complex compositional imperatives than those usual in fiction: by an *orchestration* of multiple levels of discourse, an *orchestration* which required freedom from the autonomous demands of any one level of discourse, including the chronological." Liberated from the stricture of linear chronology, the book can "express the whole random, multifarious, and fragmentary quality of experience as Sterne saw it," engaging the reader "in a perpetual guessing game" in order to keep his imagination busy and lead "death a dance." At the same time, the freedom to move rapidly from one level or type of discourse to another enables Sterne to create a sense of multiplicity and develop a satire on learning by bringing "mundane reality" into "stimulating confrontation with the furthest reaches of intellectual ingenuity and deluded pedantry."[13] Barth's own refusal to accept as a precondition the usual sequence of narrative chronology makes possible a similar kind of orchestration, permits him to blend genres in the manner of the Menippean satirist, to interrupt the linear flow of the narrative with learned digressions, philosophical dialogues, verse, and excerpts from spurious historical documents such as *The Privie Journall of Sir Henry Burlingame*. Characterized by a Shandean juxtapositioning of levels and species of discourse, *The Sot-Weed Factor* functions as a full-fledged anatomy that forces the reader to move rapidly from the elevated to the bathetic, from the sublime to the scatological, from the theoretical to the practical, and from the sacred to the profane.

The book, for instance, often seems to be a compendium of the maxim, the form which some have deprecatingly called the highest expression of eighteenth-century thought. Proverbs pepper the speech of the supposedly less educated characters such as Mary Mungummory, the Traveling Whore o'Dorset, but even Cambridge-tutored Eben, as a true man of his age, sees nothing amiss with inserting one into an argument about "Dame Chance" that also contains references to pessimistic atheism, determinism, and Hobbesian materialism and that turns upon several theological niceties (229). In another instance, Burlingame, who as a cosmophilist embraces all levels of discourse, delivers an account of his recent adventures in which he exhibits his book learning by alluding to Boetius, Solomon, and Homer while demonstrating his preference for proverbial wisdom: "Follow Horace if you will when making verse—*flebilis Ino, perfidus Ixion,* and the rest—but think not actual folk are e'er so simple. Many's the Jew hath lost his shirt, and saint that hath in private leaped his houseboy. *A covetous man may be generous on occasion,* and *Even an emmet may seek revenge*" (145).

Much of the humor in the book, of course, is a product of Eben's propensity for ignoring this advice, as he does when he and his servant Bertrand are first washed ashore. Drawing upon his knowledge

of the works of Zeno the Venetian, Peter Martyr d'Anghiera, and
Hakluyt, his familiarity with ancient maps and manuscripts, including "the antique Book of Lismore," the Laureate seeks to attach the
beach they are sitting upon to a legendary locale: "Haply 'tis Atlantis
risen from the sea, or the Sunken Land of Buss old Frobisher found;
haply 'tis Bra, whose women have much pain in bearing children, or
magic Daculi, the cradle island, where they go for gentler labor." His
less learned companion, on the other hand, feels an immediate need
to define their situation in more practical terms: " 'It matters naught
to me,' said Bertrand, 'so we be not killed by salvages. 'Tis a thing
I've feared for since we stepped ashore. Did ye read what manner of
husbands the wenches have?' " (301–2). This is relatively mild satire
a la Sterne, the not too vicious lampooning of a character's penchant
for taking hobby-horse rides. Elsewhere, however, Barth goes after erudition with a truly Rabelaisian vengeance.

At numerous points in the book abstract reasoning and scholarship
are linked to the sexual or scatological. Speaking of the knowledge he
has gained in trying to taste "every fruit the garden grows," Burlingame, for example, compares his own biological investigations with
the mathematical inquiries of his century's greatest theoretical scientist: "But ere I was twenty I knew more of the world's passions than
did Newton of its path in space. No end of *experimenta* lay behind me;
I could have writ my own *Principia* of the flesh!" (358). As he is depicted in *The Sot-Weed Factor,* Newton himself is part of an academic
community aptly described by Eben's father when he counsels his son
to undertake "an honest apprenticeship": "Cambridge my arse! 'Tis
Maryland shall be your Cambridge, and a field of sot-weed your library!" (43). According to Burlingame's version of intellectual history, Newton and his university colleague, More, are passionate
scholars who display a lust for truth that is matched only by their
lust for young lads. Their famous debate over the merits of Cartesian
philosophy is fired by their desire to win his own affections and resolved when, after "hours of colloquy," they fall "to tearful embraces"
and "move into the same lodgings," where "they would couple the
splendors of the physical world to the glories of the ideal, and listen
ravished to the music of the spheres!" (26).

Nowhere in the book, however, is learning lampooned with greater
gusto than in the passage (188–91) that describes Eben's task in "the
stables of the King o' the Seas." The Laureate's labor is less than Herculean, for, having fouled his breeches, he must simply devise a

means of cleansing himself. Searching "his education for succor, beginning with his memory of history," he consults "Herodotus, Thucydides, Polybius, Suetonius, Sallust, and other chroniclers ancient and modern" yet can "recall in them no precedent for his present plight, and thus no counsel." Next, he summons "to mind as much as ever he could of Aristotle, Epicurus, Zeno, Augustine, Thomas Aquinas, and the rest," but again fails to find a solution since philosophy deals "with generalities, categories, and abstractions alone, like More's *eternal spissitude,*" and speaks "of personal problems only insofar as they" illustrate "general ones." Rejecting "physics, astronomy, and the other areas of natural philosophy" as disciplines which are also too general in their approaches, he resolves to turn to literature and believes he has discovered a lead when he recalls "with joy that chapter out of Rabelais wherein the young Gargantua tries his hand, as it were, at sundry swabs and wipers—not in desperation, to be sure, but in a spirit of pure empiricism, to discover the noblest for good and all." But, realizing to his dismay that "(g)ood Rabelais surely meant it as a jest," he is forced to conclude that literature, too, does not "afford solutions to practical problems." Making a final effort, then, he canvasses his "knowledge of the world" and comes up emptyhanded one last time, only to discover by accident the means of his deliverance—the precious notebook that contains his *Hymn to Chastity,* a "preliminary salute to the ship *Poseidon,*" and a more than sufficient number of blank pages.

Reminiscent of Todd's bedroom epiphany and Joe Morgan's solo performance, such episodes in one sense merely carry forward the satire on abstraction and rationalism begun in the earlier works. In another sense they are the products of imitation, reflecting, as does Sterne's own skeptical treatment of "the world of learning," the "basic empiricism of the eighteenth century."[14] In *The Sot-Weed Factor,* however, the unrelenting demolition of models of the world includes even empiricism itself. Eben's frequent inability to see what lies directly in front of his face, the indeterminacy produced by metamorphosis and disguise, and Burlingame's comments about identity, flux, and the fallibility of memory all act to undermine or refute the notion that one can systematically learn from experience and experimentation. At its most subversive, Barth's satire reduces all experience of and in the world to anarchic, inconsistent relativism. Thus, even as the book "invokes some of the traditions of the English novel" in "addressing contemporary concerns," even as it develops what appears to

be an extended comparison of seventeenth-, eighteenth-, and twentieth-century world views, it sabotages this very project by suggesting that such attempts at categorization are at best fictions, at worst
ignorant or innocent oversimplifications. As the text accrues evidence,
absorbing not only actual and fictional biographies but also works of
literature and philosophy, historical documents, myths and beliefs,
what results is not general truth, but an encyclopaedia of independent
views which can be reconciled only if differences are ignored and even
then, perhaps only at the level of the cliché or maxim.

A Satire on Clio's Stage

Subject to this same differentiation and reduction, the historical
record itself becomes a collection of "privie" journals, a fabric of
fictions which have in common the depiction of the operation in time
of such basic biological factors as the territorial imperative and the
reproductive urge. Since there have been several studies made of
Barth's orchestration of historical materials in the book,[15] suffice it to
say here that in composing *The Sot-Weed Factor* he both drew upon
preexistent texts, such as Lawrence Wroth's biography of Cooke,
Cooke's own poems, and *The Archives of Maryland,* and invented
others, such as *The Privie Journal of Sir Henry Burlingame* and John
Smith's *Secret Historie of the Voiage Up the Bay of Chesapeake.* Although
the history of the historical novel since Scott may offer some justification for this method, in his apology the Author provides a more
elaborate defense of his mistreatment of "the chronicler's muse":

In the first place be it remembered, as Burlingame himself observed, that we
all invent our pasts, more or less, as we go along, at the dictates of Whim
and Interest; the happenings of former times are a clay in the present moment that will-we, nill-we, the lot of us must sculpt. . . . Moreover, this
Clio was already a scarred and crafty trollop when the Author found her. . . .
But if, despite all, he is convicted at the Public Bar of having forced what
slender virtue the strumpet may make claim to, then the Author joins with
pleasure the most engaging company imaginable, his fellow fornicators,
whose ranks include the noblest in poetry, prose, and politics. . . . (805)

Toying further with our willing suspension of disbelief in any performance enacted on "Clio's stage" (806), Barth himself has pointed out
that "most of the truly preposterous incidents in *The Sot-Weed Factor*

are based on fact," while also playfully suggesting that scholars may one day find some of his "improvisations," such as "the homosexual affair" between More and Newton, to be true, "filling in actual historical gaps."[16]

In assailing the muse's virtue, however, Barth goes beyond a simple exposition of "the rival claims of Fact and Fancy" (805). Toward the end of his story, for instance, we find Eben assuring a frightened Mrs. Russecks by speaking of "sundry theories of history," including "the retrogressive," "the dramatic," "the progressive," "the cyclical," "the undulatory," and "even the vortical," which holds "that at some non-unpredictable moment in the future the universe" will "go rigid and explode, just as the legendary bird called *Ouida* . . . was reputed to fly in ever-diminishing circles until at the end he disappeared into his own fundament" (737). What is significant about the passage is not only the obvious lampooning of theoretical models, but the fact that Eben employs such "sophistical cajolements" (737) to influence the behavior of his audience, implying something which Burlingame and Smith at times seem to believe: that the only patterns which characterize history are rhetorical patterns employed for rhetorical purposes.

When looked at from this vantage, American history in *The Sot-Weed Factor* appears to be a battleground where Platonic and Rabelaisian descriptions of the world, Cartesian and Hobbesian depictions of mankind, struggle for dominance. Both Cooke and Burlingame, of course, wish to discern a different struggle, a war between Good and Evil waged by covert combatants, such as Calvert and Coode, who exercise free will in shaping events, scripting plots and intrigues. But as the sexual and scatological overtones to Eben's rendition of the "vortical hypothesis" suggest, and as the "privie" journals Barth invents affirm, it may be that the secret factors motivating such seemingly grandiose conspiracies are nothing more, or less, than man's brutish drives, his need to propagate, his desire to possess and protect. At the level of biological cliché, *"More history's made in the bedchamber than in the throne room"* (264), and *"uneasy lies the head that wears the crown,* inasmuch as *Envy and Covetousness are ne'er satisfied"* (86).

Implicit in this assault on Clio's domain is an attack on the foundations of Jamesian realism, which proceeds from the assumptions that "the novel is history" and that the study of history is a scientific discipline. Exhibiting the fickleness of the satirist, however, Barth also

plays "fast and loose" (805) with Calliope and Polyhymnia, subjecting
the images, language, and patterns of myth and religion to the same
kind of leveling, and burlesquing both the modernist's preoccupation
with archetypes and his predecessors' fascination with types. On this
front as on the others, one strategy he employs is the purposeful violation of decorum, apparent, for instance, in Mary Mungummory's
use of mythological references, her repeated success at making "a piss-
pot o' the Holy Grail" (645), or in her description of her own, less
than immaculate, conception: "One Sabbath night whilst they knelt
in prayer he went round behind and made a mighty thrust at her;
when she cried out he explained 'twas but her final lesson in shackling
fleshly passions, and bade her go on with her prayers as if she were
in church. . . . Quick as a wink, on the words *Which art in Heav'n*,
he took her maidenhead, and if he'd a mind to commit the sin of
Onan for her protection, he had no time, for on the words *Thy kingdom come,* I was conceived" (443).

In satirizing mythological patterning, Barth, of course, uses the
traditional vehicle of parody, the most obvious examples being Eben's
stillborn epic and his attempt to incarnate the Adamic myth of America.[17] But Barth also adapts the comedy of inventory to this purpose,
particularly in the chapter entitled "A Layman's Pandect of Geminology" which presents the fruits of Burlingame's labors as comparative
mythologist. Becoming a member of the vanguard who gave birth to
this "new science" at the end of the seventeenth century and who
thereby made possible the work of Frazer, Jung, Joyce, Eliot, and
others, Burlingame had earlier joined with Eben's sister, Anna, in
undertaking "a long and secret enquiry into the subject of twins—
their place in legend, religion, and the world" (530). Although, as
he now tells Eben, the two researchers uncovered certain omnipresent
and persistent patterns, they also discovered that the patterns mean
different things to different cultures: "Sundry pairs of these twins are
opposites and sworn enemies . . . and their fight portrays the struggle of Light with Darkness, the murther of Love by Knowledge, or
what have you. Sundry others represent the equivocal state of man,
that is half angel and half beast. . . . Still others are the gods of fornication . . ." (536).

Studies such as theirs gave rise in the eighteenth century to a number of controversies about the historical or theological validity of
myth, but, even as he is burying Eben beneath a landslide of particulars, Henry tells his companion that it is "not a question of your be-

lief . . . but of the fact that other wights think it true" (534). "Aroused by his own rhetoric," Burlingame himself expresses the opinion that, no matter what twins may represent, "their union is brilliance, totality, apocalypse," and that it is his desire to experience *"in coito"* this "jointure of polarities" that explains his lust for Eben and Anna (536–37). It may be impossible to determine whether he actually reverences "the act of fornication as portraying the fruitful union of opposites" (533) or merely employs the language of mythology to portray his love of fornication. What his success at convincing both himself and Eben does make clear, however, is that mythological patterns and images can be powerful rhetorical tools—indeed, soon after Burlingame concludes his speech within sight of a ship called *Pilgrim,* he takes possession of Eben's revised *Marylandiad* and sends it to one of his agents, as if to remind us of the connection between the myth of America and other more martial and political expressions of "manifest destiny."

Barth's own pandect of geminology is, obviously, a good deal more comprehensive than Burlingame's, contains many more examples of the "mystery of twos and ones" (533), including such duos as Calvert and Coode, who are viewed by some as devil and demigod; Anna and Joan, who as aspects of the female archetype wear the labels Virgin and Whore; and Eben and Henry themselves, who at times fade into one of the most recurrent pairs of character types in literature: a tall, thin, fanciful man and a shorter, plumper, more worldly one. Playing roles filled before them by Don Quixote and Sancho Panza, Walter and Toby Shandy, they constitute what Barth calls the "mainspring" of the book's "philosophical and emotional dramas."[18] Time and again, their interaction releases energy and humor as they are pulled apart by misunderstanding and conflicting opinions, only to be wound tightly together once more by the force of genuine affection.

The conflict between their world views, between Burlingame's Heraclitean cosmophilism and Eben's Platonic essentialism, is also a clash of aesthetics. Were he an artist, Burlingame would carve "the living truth" as it exists, "make love" in verse to all of material creation (355). On the other hand, although Eben possesses a "sense of the arbitrariness of the particular real world," he is unwilling to submit to "its finality," cannot accept the fact that France will "have to go on resembling a teapot forever" (9). As a result, he begins by living in other worlds, spinning out alternate histories, and even after he is made to concede that "the poet must fling himself into the arms of Life" to avoid the paralysis of cosmopsis, he still maintains that he must also "hide his heart away and ne'er surrender it," "shake free" of the world he is born to "ere it shackle him" (511–12). Both his satiric rejection of his estate and the epitaph he composes for himself suggest that he never fully rejects this position, never finds it possible completely to resist the attractions of "Fancy's chast Couch."

But while we may be thus encouraged to view Eben and Henry as types, as the embodiments of antithetical philosophical or aesthetic positions, they, like the Shandy brothers, "are humorous characters, not embodied humours,"[19] and Barth not only gives us cause to wonder about his own type casting but also refuses to resolve the dialectic he creates. Both Cooke and Burlingame wish, perhaps, to believe that they are characters whose behavior is dominated by a single psychological tendency or world view, yet both are prevented from consistently and convincingly playing these roles by the arbitrary dictates of *"wanton Nature, void of Rest"* (136). Eben's lust and virility, amply displayed in the *Cyprian* incident, challenge his belief in the simplicity and purity of his essence, and he is forced by circumstances to choose to violate his own innocence. Except when the problem is temporarily remedied by means of the eggplant recipe, Henry's anatomical shortcoming makes impossible the full physical expression of his cosmophily, and, although he claims "God's whole creation" as "his mistress" (354), in order to avoid madness, he must "assert," "quill his name on the universe" (373), and by shaping the world limit his boundless love to the infatuation of a Pygmalion with a Galatea. Moreover, since Burlingame alters his appearance to conceal his identity and Cooke takes on an identity to conceal the fact that he is "consistently no special sort of person" (12), both are in a sense chameleons. Their proclivity for changing shapes and personalities, along with all the other examples of metamorphosis in the book, not only contradicts the notion that they are character types but calls into question the usefulness of thinking in terms of types and archetypes, the validity of our very conceptions of "likeness" and "difference."

Given this, it is certainly not surprising that we find nothing in the account of their ultimate fates to indicate unequivocally the sufficiency or superiority of either man's world view. As Barth has pointed out, paradoxically it is Eben, "the figure who begins as a kind of naïf and a more or less impotent and ineffectual man" who "turns out to be the one who finally has what potency there is in the novel,"[20] siring *The Sot-Weed Factor,* earning Malden by consummating his marriage with Joan. Each act involves the loss of a kind of innocence, but it is not necessarily true that in losing his virginity he learns the lesson of his tutor, becomes a convert to cosmophily. Demonstrating that there is "no perfect educational method" (9), Eben, for the most part, spends the remainder of his life cultivating his own garden in relative isolation, his disposing of his estate, his delusion that Nicholas Lowe is Burlingame, and his final rejection of Fame in favor of Fancy and Jesus all indicating that his gaze is focused not on this world, but on other ones.

Synthesis, as well, is denied us, for Barth has stated that he is "not sure" it is "possible," and "not terribly interested in it anyhow." Burlingame's act of *"atonement"* (533), involving the fusion of intellectual, sexual, and mythic opposites, never becomes more than an "imagined union . . . at the end of the dramatic dialectic,"[21] and as the mainspring winds down, the two characters travel separate ways, exhausting their remaining possibilities and losing the battle with entropy. Made "fond" by "age" (817), Ebenezer succumbs to a quinsy, and he and his work are relegated to obscurity awaiting Barth's resurrection of both of them. Immersing himself a final time in the flux of experience, the play of events, the muddle of conspiracies, Henry is absorbed into the welter of history, reappearing only in the form of a delusion.

Thus, if the conflict of ideas is never resolved, history shown to be fictional and myth limited, if all systems of learning are satirized and we discover nothing which has any predictive value, what, then, does *The Sot-Weed Factor* offer us? Does Barth invoke the tradition of the English novel merely to place us, with Eben, in the stables of the King o' the Seas?

For one thing, by masterfully combining wit with humor, Barth provides us with one of the eighteenth century's favorite antidotes for spleen. At times we are made self-conscious about our response, as when we hear the story of Charley Mattassin, who commits murder as a jest and chuckles all the way to the gallows. But though there exist several such examples of laughter in the dark, there is also a great deal in the book that is simply and genuinely funny.

For another thing, we are made to feel. To be sure, Barth's world is not the protected microcosm of *Tristram Shandy* where one can safely believe in benevolence and sensibility; there is too much pain and loss, too much vice and cruelty. We may, however, share in the affection between Eben and his tutor, we are often afforded the satisfaction of sensing our indignation rise at the sight of inhumanity and injustice, and, if Barth is again successful in reorchestrating the elements of farce and satire "to get at some of the passion and power of the tragic view of life," we may even experience something akin to catharsis.

Beyond this, we are offered the pleasure of following "a tale well wrought," the "gossip of the gods" (636–37), and permitted for a time to exist in a Maryland, a border state, where "the rival claims of Fact and Fancy" may be overridden "with fair impunity" (805) and the competing aesthetics of Cooke and Burlingame need not be reconciled. Blending story and history to foster a basic distrust of systematic thinking and generate a plot that is incredibly complex yet neatly and arbitrarily concluded, Barth manages to give expression once more to the attitude of satire while also feeding our curiosity and fulfilling our desire for completion. Employing "historical imitation" and orchestration to produce a "formal farce"[22] in which literary conventions are rejuvenated and language is liberated to play freely, he creates the illusion of novelty and plenitude while providing patterns that satisfy our need for order.

To the critic who still remains discontented one may only cite Eben's defense of his own fiction:

What moral doth the story hold? Is't that the universe is vain? The chaste and consecrated a hollow madness? Or is't that what the world lacks we must ourselves supply? My brave assault on Maryland—this knight-errantry of Innocence and Art—sure, I see now 'twas an edifice raised not e'en on sand, but on the black and vasty zephyrs of the Pit. Wherefore a voice in me cries, "Down with't, then!" while another stands in awe before the enterprise; sees in the vanity of't all nobleness allowed to fallen men. (680)

Chapter Five
Why Must We Sing This Refrain Again?

Menippean Satire and Monomyth

If *The Sot-Weed Factor* may be characterized as anatomy masquerading as historical novel or bildungsroman, then *Giles Goat-Boy* is a Menippean satire that has assumed the form of allegory or sacred text.[1] As Frye puts it, a "writer is being allegorical whenever it is clear that he is saying 'by this I *also* (*allos*) mean that.' If this seems to be done continuously, we may say, cautiously, that what he is writing 'is' an allegory. In *The Faerie Queene*, for instance, the narrative systematically refers to historical examples and the meaning to moral precepts, besides doing their own work in the poem. Allegory, then, is a contrapuntal technique, like canonical imitation in music."[2] Described by Barth as "a comic Old Testament" possessing an "intricate structure" suggestive of "musical form," *Giles* seems to function as "canonical imitation" in several senses of the term.[3]

The basic pattern informing the narrative of Barth's "Revised New Syllabus" is that of the "monomyth" elaborated by comparative mythologists such as Campbell and Raglan. Barth composed variations upon this "formal pattern," he has said, because he finds it a fascinating "phenomenon," because it is "one of the most profound notions that the human mind has come up with," one of the most magnificent edifices fallen men have raised over the blackness of the Pit.[4] As the story of the Goat-Boy's efforts to prove himself a Grand Tutor takes on the shape of the archetypal hero's quest for enlightenment and self-discovery, the narrative also systematically refers, by means of rather obvious correspondences, to contemporary figures and events and the meaning to philosophical positions and moral precepts, or, more precisely, to the epistemological bases of ethical and religious belief.

The world of *Giles Goat-Boy* is a blatant lie, a Wonderland or Laputa the particulars of which are determined by a single "controlling metaphor" that is also a play on words: the universe is a university. In creating the Floating Opera and Wicomico State, employing tidewater Maryland as an "emblem for other sorts of border states," Barth had made setting serve metaphorical ends before. In none of his first three works, however, is the conceit so elaborate and encompassing as to constitute this kind of adventure in ordering; in none of them is it used, as it is in *Giles*, as the primary means of escaping "the *literal* contemporary" in order to "beat the realistic thing."[5]

To foster the illusion of temporal relocation, Barth wrote *The Sot-Weed Factor* in imitation eighteenth-century prose. To transport us to the Goat-Boy's alternate university, he concocted a unique and dislocating narrative voice:

George is my name; my deeds have been heard of in Tower Hall, and my childhood has been chronicled in the *Journal of Experimental Psychology*. I am he that was called in those days Billy Bocksfuss—cruel misnomer. For had I indeed a cloven foot I'd not hobble upon a stick or need ride pick-a-back to class in humid weather. Aye, it was just for want of a proper hoof that in my fourteenth year I was the kicked instead of the kicker; that I lay crippled on the reeking peat and saw my first love tupped by a brute Angora. Mercy on that buck who butted me from one world to another; whose fell horns turned my sweetheart's fancy, drove me from the pasture, and set me gimping down the road I travel yet. This bare brow, shame of my kidship, I crowned with the shame of men: I bade farewell to my hornless goathood and struck out, a hornèd human student, for Commencement Gate.[6]

This voice, which we may or may not presume to be that of the Goat-Boy himself, is both distinctive and eclectic. It is a satyric voice that mixes the vocabulary of the barnyard with the jargon of academe and consistently combines the sacred with the profane, continuously reminding us of the speaker's dualistic nature, of the principle that "proctoscopy repeats hagiography" (43). Embedding Anglicisms ("tupped") in a substrate that generally sounds like American English, blending topical allusions, the "university" equivalent of contemporary slang, and language more archaic in flavor ("Aye," "hornèd"), it is a voice that cannot be located in space and time.

George's habitual inversion of normal syntax and his fondness for stilted locutions and elevated diction are stylistic characteristics that suggest an affinity between his "Revised New Syllabus" and English translations of classical epics or the King James Version of the Bible. Moreover, he often employs formulas that seem to be designed to establish his credentials as savior or mythic hero. "I am he," he says when describing how he had been made into a scapegoat, appropriating the phrase used by Christ to identify himself as the Messiah. "George is my name; my deeds have been heard of in Tower Hall . . . ," he tells us, adopting the formula Odysseus follows as he begins recounting his heroic adventures to Alcinoüs. These are the words of one who believes, or is pretending to believe, that he is different from other men, that he has lived a life of mythic proportions or has proved himself the singular individual whose life is a fulfillment of prophecy.

But while the way the Goat-Boy says things may at times indicate that his actions and abilities are unparalleled or that he is the unique antitype prefigured by a series of antecedent types, at other times his use of figurative language implies that his life is the embodiment of recurrent patterns and that he himself is not an individual but an archetype:

Seven years I spent a-prepping—where did they fly? It is an interval in my history far from clear. As those unlettered hordes of old swept down on the halls of Remus College and were civilized by what they sacked, so vandal youth must bring forever the temple of its heritage to rubble, and turning then the marble shatters in its hand, commence to wonder and grow wise, regret its ignorance, and call at last for mortarbox and trowel. Just such a reconstruction was that account of my earliest years, whose cracks and plaster-fills will not have escaped the critical; and such another must I render now of my education, like an archaeologist his lost seminaries of antiquity, from its intellectual residue. (113)

In linking his story, history, and what is "forever" true, George apparently is demonstrating here the validity of what is referred to in the book as "Spielman's Law," the theory that *"ontogeny recapitulates cosmogeny,"* the concept that "our Founder on Founder's Hill and the rawest freshman on his first *mons veneris* are father and son," that "my day, my year, my life, and the history of West Campus are wheels within wheels" (43).

This, of course, is the governing principle of *Finnegans Wake*, in which, if the reader wishes, HCE becomes not only a fictional Irish publican but legions of literary and historical figures, mythic heroes, and Eastern and Western deities, not merely a mortal human being but an Everyman who takes on the qualities of the masculine aspect of the godhead itself. As Joyce's work illustrates, "Spielman's Law" can form the basis of an effective strategy for combatting exhaustion. By means of the dream language Joyce invented, *Finnegans Wake* explodes out of the confines of literary realism as virtually endless chains of association are generated and specific characters, settings, and times linked to a multiplicity of people, places, and ages. Although *Giles* is not composed in Joycean "portmanteau" language, the eclectic nature of George's speech creates, if to a lesser degree, similar effects. Furthermore, the reader is encouraged by the Goat-Boy's reference to Spielman's theory and by his use of figurative language to believe that there is a historical or mythic analogue for everything he says about himself, to conceive of his narrative as a kind of contrapuntal composition in which George's voice evokes by implication the other voices of the canonical imitation, contributing further to the impression of plenitude.

For Joseph Campbell, whose work Barth consulted in devising his own version of the "monomyth,"[7] the principle that "ontogeny recapitulates cosmogeny" is not merely a convenient conceit but the basic truth taught by mythology. According to Campbell, the mythological adventure of the archetypal hero who is each of us is a "perfect microcosmic mirror of the macrocosm," and the mythic hero and "his ultimate god, the seeker and the found" are to be "understood as the outside and inside of a single, self-mirrored mystery, which is the mystery of the manifest world." Furthermore, "to grasp the full value of the mythological figures" from various cultures "we must understand that they are not only symptoms of the unconscious . . . but also controlled and intended statements of certain spiritual principles which have remained as constant through the course of human history as the form and nervous structure of the human physique itself."[8]

Giles Goat-Boy not only imitates in minute detail the cyclical pattern of the quest of the hero but also passes itself off as an "encyclopaedic" work structured by the "monomyth," as an imitation Bible, *Divina Commedia*, or *Faerie Queene*. As Frye defines it, an "encyclopaedic" work is one that is primarily "thematic" in nature (i.e., one in which "the primary interest is in *dianoia*, the idea or poetic thought") produced by a poet acting as "a spokesman of his society" and articulating "a poetic knowledge and expressive power which is latent or needed" in that society. Conceived as being "a sacred book" or some other "analogy of revelation," the "encyclopaedic" text is to be viewed as an expression of a "total body of vision that poets as a whole are entrusted with." The task of giving form to this totality "can be at-

tempted by one poet if he is sufficiently learned or inspired or by a
poetic school or tradition if the culture is sufficiently homogeneous."
"Encyclopaedic" works of different ages and modes are informed by
different concepts of the source and nature of the poet's vision and
authority.[9]

Because it plays variations upon the journey of the archetypal ques-
tor, we may be tempted to read *Giles* in the way some read *Finnegans
Wake*, as an expression of the psychological and spiritual principles
that Campbell believes are conveyed by the pattern. But Barth has
indicated that he is "not the least bit interested in the truth or false-
hood of the various explanations of the so-called mono-myth," not
convinced that "Jung is right about the 'collective unconscious.' " (To
emphasize the point, he has wryly stated that Campbell "may be a
crank" for all he knows or cares.)[10] Because "The Revised New Syllabus" imitates a number of texts that may be labeled as sacred books
or analogies of revelation, we may be led to infer that the voice that
narrates it is a vehicle for visionary truth, drawing upon one or more
of the sources of authority associated with encyclopedic works.
Throughout the book, however, Barth toys with our conceptions of
inspiration, context, and authorial intention, employing as one of
several means to this end the reorchestration of yet another literary
convention, the narrative frame.

The Narrative Frame

George's narrative, consisting of "The Revised New Syllabus"
proper and a "Posttape" in which he questions the value of both his
revelation and his quest, is bracketed proximately by two notes attributed to one "J. B." The first of these, a "Cover-Letter To The
Editors and Publisher," makes use of "a novelistic standby," the "Authorial pretense that his manuscript is a factual chronicle inadvertently happened upon."[11] After describing the course of his love affair
with "the Muse," J. B. asserts that, like Eben, he has now "caught
Knowledge like a love-pox," has been transformed from "a monger
after Beauty" to "a priest of Truth" (xxi–xxii) as a result of encountering a mysterious stranger whom he presumes to be the son of one
George Giles, a *"professor extraordinarius"* whose unorthodox methods
and ideas had won him a number of devoted protégés before he disappeared off the face of the earth (xxxi). Wishing to correct the discrep-
ancies and contradictions in the accounts of his father's life and work

produced by these followers, "Stoker Giles" allegedly began reading
their manuscripts into an automatic computer named WESCAC that
"not only pointed out in accordance with its program the hopeless
disagreement of the texts," but also assembled, collated, and edited
the "considerable original matter" in its memory banks, combining
it with "all verifiable data from other sources such as the memoirs"
to compose "a coherent narrative from the Grand Tutor's point of
view" (xxxii). This material was then read out in "an elegant form"
on WESCAC's "automatic printers," to create the supposedly authoritative text entitled "The Revised New Syllabus," delivered by Stoker
Giles to J. B. and subsequently submitted by the latter for publication.

The similarities between this "Cover-Letter" and "The Custom
House" are rather obvious, but whereas Hawthorne's claim that *The
Scarlet Letter* is based upon a documentary account of actual, verifiable
events conjures an historical context for allegory while permitting
him to pretend that he is assuming the authority of the chronicler, J.
B.'s missive fails in its ostensible efforts to establish a context, undermines the authority and authenticity of the document it presents, and
"inadvertently" suggests the possibility that the "Truth" embodied in
Giles's "encyclopaedic" text has been arrived at by a committee operating under the aegis of Fancy. While proposing that *"The Revised
New Syllabus* is the work not of 'WESCAC' but of an obscure, erratic
wizard whose *nom de plume* is *Stoker, Giles"* (xxxvi), J. B. admits that
there are other possibilities, including, presumably, the one espoused
by certain "Gilesians" who believe the "encyclopaedic" work to be a
medium for "the GILES's very voice," a conduit for the inspired wisdom of an oracular "Grand Tutor" (xxxiii). To accept the former pretense is to become reconciled to the impossibility of ascribing any
particular kind of authority to the document's elusive author, in
which case the reader must be satisfied with his own assessment of
the value of "the book's wisdom" (xxxvi) or with his evaluation of its
worth as artifact. To accept the other is to view "The Revised New
Syllabus" as a product of joint authorship, consisting not only of the
"original matter" composed by the "Grand Tutor" and the commentary provided by his followers but also the corrections and additions
made by WESCAC (programmed, presumably, by someone), the
changes introduced "here and there" by young Stoker (xxxii), and
"certain emendations and re-arrangements which the Author's imper-

fect mastery of our idiom and his avowed respect" for J. B.'s "artistic judgement encouraged" the latter "to make" (xxxvi).

The integrity of the text is further called into question in the second of the appendages attributed to J. B., the "Postscript to the Posttape." Entering the labyrinth of textual criticism, the "aspirant professor of Gilesianism" attempts to demonstrate that the "Posttape" is a spurious document not consistent with the "Grand Tutor's" intent, an "interpolation of later Gilesians, perhaps—more likely of antigilesians—or an improvisation of *Wescacus malinoctis*, but not the scripture, so to speak, of George Giles" (765). Although J. B. offers evidence for his evaluation, he discloses that his rejection of the "Posttape" depends, ultimately, on his conception of the "Grand Tutor's" doctrine, his subjective sense of such intangibles as "tone." Although he quickly circumvents the implications of his own statements, he raises the possibility that the act of interpreting not only the "Syllabus" but "all artistic and pedagogical conceit," "especially of the parable kind," constitutes a "translation" of the work into "our terms" (766). The frame provided by J. B., then, is, among other things, a parody of scriptural exegesis that suggests that "encyclopaedic" texts viewed in one context as representing literal truth may in another be read as allegories (exemplified, for instance, by the church fathers' reinterpreting the Old Testament in terms of typology), that any extended interpretation is an allegorization of the text, and that the belief that eclectic "sacred books" such as "The Revised New Syllabus" are uniform expressions of revealed truth rests upon the assumption that the entire process of their composition, including the efforts of editors and translators, must be viewed as inspired.

The material provided us by J. B. is itself contained within another frame, made up of a "Publisher's Disclaimer" and a "Footnote to the Postscript to the Posttape." The latter simply notes that the type of J. B.'s "Postscript" is not the same as that of his "Cover-Letter," raising doubts about the authenticity of both. The former is a much more elaborate pretense that, under the guise of recording a disagreement among editors about the merits of publishing the manuscript, offers the potential reader a handful of preprogrammed responses to the work as well as several differing perceptions of its author's intentions. Regardless of their final estimations of the book's literary and, more important, pecuniary worth, editors *A* through *D* agree that it is "unrealistic," rejects "what *is the case*" in favor of the "preposter-

ous" and "absurd," and may even be a perverse and liberating "hoax."
Taken as a whole, this body of criticism delivers the same message
conveyed to us by "THE EDITOR-IN-CHIEF," that the "reader must begin this book with an act of faith and end it with an act of charity,"
reading and believing "what he pleases" (xi–xix).

"One Can't Transmit Knowledge"

Barth has stated that his "notion of the way to make fiction, correctly, carefully, is to make every possible aspect of the fiction resonate, reflect, emblemize the main concerns of the fiction: your choice
of place, your choice of viewpoint, your choice of language, your
choice of cadence, your choice of punctuation, your cast of characters,
your whole aesthetic premises about writing the fiction in so far as
you have enough intelligence to be aware of them, and imagine them,
and put them to use."[12] In *Giles Goat-Boy* not only the narrative
frames but also Barth's version of the "monomyth," his reorchestration of Greek tragedy, and even the controlling metaphor that deter-
mines to a large extent the particulars of setting and the qualities of
the language all "emblemize" or "resonate" a basic theme: "one can't
transmit knowledge."[13] Although *Giles* imitates a number of sacred
books and passes itself off as a work primarily concerned with *dianoia,*
Barth goes to a great deal of trouble to both burlesque the kinds of
authority traditionally associated with "encyclopaedic" works and undermine his own authority to serve as a spokesman for his society capable of articulating poetic knowledge. *Giles* seems to function like
an allegory, but whereas the allegorist must make it clear that he is
saying "by this I also mean that," Barth merely asserts "when I say
this I am at the same time saying that."

The patterns that make up Barth's contrapuntal composition are
never coincident with one another and are brought into correspondence only through George's conscious efforts to imitate or as a result
of the trope-making abilities of the narrative voice and the reader
himself. George's journey replicates the basic pattern of the "monomyth" and he may even experience what he interprets as a moment
of apotheosis, but the experience cannot be communicated and he fails
to complete the mythic passage from tragedy to comedy. Unlike
Campbell's "mythological hero" who sees life to be "penetrated by an
all-suffusing, all-sustaining love, and a knowledge of its own uncon-
quered power,"[14] George remains finally unconvinced that he and the

undying god are one and the same, becomes ambivalent about the knowledge that "ontogeny recapitulates cosmogeny" and all is governed by the "Law of Cyclology"(41). If he feels, at least momentarily, that he has arrived at truth, it is not a truth that is embodied in any single one of the religious, philosophical, or ethical systems he encounters or that represents a synthesis of all of them. Nor do his actions, ultimately, have a lasting effect upon his society or upon the history of "the University"—as we discover in the "Posttape," "The Boundary Dispute" between "East-Campus" and "West-Campus" remains unresolved, for he has failed to redeem the future of "studentdom," exorcise the spectre of "Campus Riot III."

Like the "endless tapes" on which "The Revised New Syllabus" is supposed to be recorded, the pattern of the "monomyth" is presumed to be a closed loop:

Cycles on cycles, ever unwinding: like my watch; like the reels of the machine she got past her spouse; like the University itself.
    Unwind, rewind, replay. (755)

But, whereas the abstract pattern may be repeated mechanically ad infinitum, the Goat-Boy assumes that his particular quest will terminate in his death: "Late or soon, we lose. Sudden or slow, we lose. The bank exacts its charge for each redistribution of our funds. There is an entropy to time, a tax on change: four nickels for two dimes, but always less silver; our books stay reconciled, but who in modern terms can tell heads from tails?" (763). Since the pattern of references in the text to moral or philosophical precepts is one in which contradiction terminates time and again in paradox, the historical and topical allusions that start to emerge once the reader begins to interpret the work allegorically become solutions to an extended guessing game that terminates in exhaustion. In guiding us, thus, along certain avenues of allegorical interpretation, ways of arriving at the moral and anagogic or universal meaning of the fiction, only to lead us into the culs-de-sac at the ends of those roads, *Giles Goat-Boy*, of course, emulates not the great analogies of revelation produced by Dante, Spenser, and Milton, but the great satires of Rabelais, Petronius, and Apuleius.

According to Frye, in "the riotous chaos" of works such as *The Golden Ass*, *Gargantua and Pantagruel*, or *Finnegans Wake*, the satirist

achieves a "final victory" not only over learning and systems of belief
but over "common sense" as well:

When we have finished with their weirdly logical fantasies of debauch,
dream, and delirium we wake up wondering if Paracelsus' suggestion is right
that the things seen in delirium are really there, like stars in daytime, and
invisible for the same reason. Lucius becomes initiated and slips evasively out
of our grasp, whether he lied or told the truth, as St. Augustine says with
a touch of exasperation; Rabelais promises us a final oracle and leaves us staring at an empty bottle; Joyce's HCE struggles for pages toward wakening,
but just as we seem on the point of grasping something tangible we are
swung around to the first page of the book again. The *Satyricon* is a torn
fragment from what seems like a history of some monstrous Atlantean race
that vanished in the sea, still drunk.[15]

In like manner, Barth provides us with characters and events that
seem to allude to and illuminate contemporary and historical examples, only to end up suggesting that our reflections are goatish, that
George's world and ours are both insane, offers, if facetiously, to initiate us into the mysteries, teach us metaphysical truths or convey
practical wisdom, only to refocus our attention on the literal meaning
and creative energy of George's incredible and often discreditable narrative. As "Editor D" puts it in the "Publisher's Disclaimer": "We
had asked for revelations; he palms off his maddest dreams. 'Show us
Beauty,' we plead; he bares his rump to us. 'Show us Goodness,' we
beg, and he mounts our wives and daughters. 'Ah, sir!' we implore
him, 'Give us the Truth!' He thrusts up a forefinger from each temple
and declares, 'You are cuckolds all' " (xix).

In terms of *dianoia*, then, *Giles Goat-Boy* may seem to some to be
nothing more or less than a particularly complex and engaging
"shaggy goat" story that assimilates ideas, ideologies, and dogmas in
circling back to where it began. Taking the gullible reader on an
"epic quest for Answers" (43), it rewards him by, in effect, delivering
as punch lines a group of deflating dicta he had encountered early on,
dicta that apparently mock his inquisitivenes and reduce mystery to
physiology, the soteriological to the scatological: *"Self-knowledge is always bad news"* (121); the Riddle of the Sphinx and "the 'sphincter's
riddle' " are one and the same; "proctoscopy repeats hagiography"
(43). Since he has been amply cautioned against expecting anything
else by the comments of the text's imaginary editors, the tone of

George's narration, and the obvious presence of farcical elements in the narrative, the reader who completes this journey has permitted himself to be mocked thus, has for a number of reasons willingly allowed himself to be gulled. For one thing, even though he may be convinced of the futility of attempting systematically to derive kinds of meanings other than the "literal" (the account of what happens), may realize that what he is experiencing is not thematically a type of canonical imitation but a single melody, he may find that melody sufficiently intriguing to warrant his attention. George's story, after all, is an extremely complex variation on the most popular plot of all time, and what happens in it is often salacious or sensational enough to bring out the goat in the most jaded of readers. In addition, no matter how it performs *thematically*, how thoroughly it expresses the attitude of satire, *Giles* is *formally* a contrapuntal composition that, like *Finnegans Wake*, incorporates elements of all four forms of fiction defined by Frye—the novel, romance, confession, and anatomy.[16] A certain type of reader may delight in perceiving the intricacy with which these elements are interwoven, may find pleasure in discovering that even minute details contribute to the unity of the book's design. This, of course, is the way many people engage Joyce's work, turning the reading experience into an act of appreciation and an exercise in self-congratulation. In such cases, criticism becomes analogous to scriptural exegesis, the reader may see himself as an acolyte or adept, and the author has regained something like the authority possessed by the authors of earlier "encyclopaedic" texts, for, regardless of whether or not he is viewed as a seer or spokesman, he is considered to be a consummate maker.

Barth, certainly, has often indicated that he attaches a kind of value to pure story and pure design. Yet he has also stated that he aspires to "passionate virtuosity" and that his "motive" in writing *Giles* was "to begin with a travesty or parody, but then hopefully to escalate it to something more passionate." Moreover, referring us to "the old spurious etymology of the words *tragedy* and *satire*, both of which have been traced back to the root word for goat," he has described that passion as "tragic."[17]

Although George attempts to prove himself a "Grand Tutor," a saint or savior capable of transcending human limitations and redeeming history and studentdom, he is throughout associated with tragic heroes such as Adam and Oedipus. Raised as a goat under the protection of Max Spielman, he spends his "kidhood" in a condition of timeless, animal innocence and pragmatic simplicity:

My moral training required no preachment (not the least respect in which it differed absolutely from that of humans): Who neglects his appetites suffers their pangs; Who presumes incautiously may well be butted; Who fouls his stall must sleep in filth. Cleave to him, I learned, who does you kindness; Avoid him who does you hurt; Stay inside the fence; Take of what's offered as much as you can for as long as you may; Don't exchange the certain for the possible; Boss when you're able, be bossed when you aren't, but don't forsake the herd. Simple lessons, instinct with wisdom, that grant to him who heeds them afternoons of blowsy bliss and dreamless nights. (45)

With the growth of lust and self-awareness, this existence comes to an end for him—in a fit of rage and jealousy he raises himself erect to kill a rival ram, and, experiencing guilt and loss after the fact, learns he is human.

His discovery that he is a human being does not lead immediately, however, to an acceptance of being human, for in "all of goatdom" Homo sapiens is the only creature capable of tricking himself (147). The Goat-Boy's fall into self-knowledge is forestalled because the "buck who" butts him "from one world to another," expels him "from the pasture" and sets him "gimping down the road" of studenthood, merely drives him from a state of goatish ignorance to a state of human innocence. His fancy awakening with his consciousness, he refuses to accept the natural order of things:

At best I found it moderately poetic that every action had an equal and opposite reaction, or that an embryo's gestation repeated the evolution of its phylum; for the most part I regarded natural laws with the same provisional neutrality with which one regards the ground-rules of a game or the exposition of a fable, and the reflection that one had no choice of games whatever (when so many others were imaginable) could bring me on occasion to severe melancholy. Indeed, if I never came truly to despair at the awful arbitrariness of Facts, it was because I never more than notionally accepted them. (117)

Lacking experience, he is still capable of convincing himself of his "utter freedom": "surely there would be other roles in other realms, an endless succession of names and natures. . . . Nothing for me was simply *the case* forever and aye, only '*this* case' " (117).

But as the Goat-Boy himself continues to evolve, he inevitably begins to acquire an unsettling knowledge of things as they are. He is disturbed by Oedipal dreams that, in arousing both lust and guilt, suggest Max may be correct in asserting that "Every man's part goat and part Grand Tutor" (119), that human existence is dualistic, that there is no escaping either one's brutish needs or the need to escape them. Truly *"seeing"* his tutor's face "for the first time," he becomes aware of, and is repelled by, the possibility that a man's freedom may be limited, his life, like that of any organism, temporally bounded: "Here was this growth called Max, utterly other than myself, with shaggy white hair and withered body and quiet old voice; with feelings and life of its own, whose history, nearly finished, consisted of such-and-such events and no others. He had done *A*, *B*, and *C*; *X* and *Y* had been done to him; *Z*, his little fate, lay just ahead. Max . . . existed! He was, had been, and would for a while yet be a *person*, truly as I" (123). "How can a person stand it, not to be . . . marvelous?" he wonders, the thought that Max's "reality" might become his own filling him with "a woozy repugnance" (123).

Deciding that there is no "point in being human" if all he "can be is a regular person" (123), he, like Eben, names himself and chooses to prove himself "less than mortal and more," to reject "the faun" in him (150) and demonstrate that he is "Wisdom and Goodness Incarnate" (138). Not satisfied with "Being" (which in one of the book's contexts has sexual connotations) he commits himself to becoming a "Grand Tutor," to solving the riddle, arriving at "the Answer" that will liberate all of studentdom from natural law. In choosing to affirm his liberty thus, George, like Milton's Adam, uses "freedom to lose freedom." As Frye points out, "just as comedy often sets up an arbitrary law and then organizes the action to break or evade it, so tragedy presents the reverse theme of narrowing a comparatively free life into a process of causation. This happens to Macbeth when he accepts the logic of usurpation, to Hamlet when he accepts the logic of revenge, to Lear when he accepts the logic of abdication."[18]

In accepting the logic of "Grand-Tutorhood," George agrees to submit to a teleological process and to reduce self-definition to a single propositional statement. He must undertake a journey to New Tammany College and undergo the trials that will determine whether he either is or is not the "GILES" ("Grand-tutorial Ideal, Laboratory Eugenical Specimen"). If he is successfully initiated in the "Belly" of the omnipotent computer WESCAC, he may be able to liberate studentdom from its fear of being "EATen" (subjected to Electroencephalic Amplification and Transmission, to a "mental burn-out" that is "terminable" only "by the death of the victim"), but to accomplish this goal he must change the computer's AIM (Automatic Implementation Mechanism), alter the programming of the University, the laws of his universe.

None of the systems of thought or belief that George encounters en route or on campus is sufficient to show him the way, for he learns what the Menippean satirist believes, that any system is an oversimplification of experience, discovers that one may negate any given stance by conceiving an equally defensible contradictory position. Formal "course-work," he learns, can not help him with his "Assignment," for, plunging into the "learned chatter" of "books and lectures," one quickly becomes lost in an endless maze of glosses upon glosses upon glosses (443–55). Finding such received schemata "unpalatable," the Goat-Boy resolves to "wrest" his own "Answers like swede-roots by main strength from their holes" (455), to fulfill his tasks by attacking polarity and contradiction head-on, confronting the concepts of likeness and difference.

Twice, solution-in-head, he enters the bowels of the computer to be tested. The first time, he offers an "Answer" that has been variously described by critics as "Western" and "rational," as an affirmation of "the principle of analysis," of "differentiation"; the second time an "Answer" that has been called "Eastern," an "inversion of reason," a negation of differentiation leading to a "union of contraries."[19] In both cases he comes to see that he has failed; when both stances are translated into programs for altering what is the case, the consequences are nearly disastrous. Therefore, together with Anastasia, virgin and whore, Queen of Heaven and bride of Hades, he descends into the "Belly" a third time, feeling that he now understands his "nature and function" "quite clearly and disinterestedly" (728). Embracing each other and coupling "*Input*" and "*Output*" (730), they respond in a manner that has been termed a "Synthesis," a " 'transcension of categories' as well as, or through the 'union of contraries,' " "a Taoistic 'letting be,' distinguished by spontaneity and carelessness," an "Answer" that "collapses" and "embraces" both previous "Answers."[20] Discovering "in Anastasia" the "University whole and clear," George sees or envisions it as "an entire, single, seamless campus" in which "*Here* lay with *there*, *tick* clipped *tock*, *all* serviced *nothing*; I and My Ladyship, all, were one" (731).

Are we to interpret this as a description of mythic initiation, a mystical marriage of hero and goddess leading to atonement and enlightenment, to the understanding that, as Campbell puts it, "the sickening and insane tragedies of this vast and ruthless cosmos are completely validated in the majesty of Being"?[21] Or are we to respond the way we do when Henry Burlingame speaks of atonement, of his reverence for the act of fornication as representing the union of contraries? Is what the words denote transcendence or merely sexual transport? When George says "I fed myself myself" (731), is the reference to "at-one-ment" or to solipsism? As he short-circuits both WESCAC and his own self-consciousness and he and Anastasia die in each other's arms in "that fell, Commencèd place" (732), does he know apotheosis or gain foreknowledge of that which Hamlet called "a consummation devoutly to be wished," embrace Being or the freedom of annihilation?

If we can believe what George tells us, then we must also believe that he cannot tell us. The experience, he says, is "unspeakable! Unnamable! Unimaginable!" (709). If the mystical has become manifest, it cannot be put into words. As Oedipus informs Theseus near the conclusion of the second play of Sophocles' trilogy, there are mysteries that cannot be explained, for one must arrive at them alone.

Having reached the climax of his quest, George discovers a certain freedom to Be. Having come to an acceptance of his goatishness, he can, in a sense, retrace his way, "joyfully" romp with a descendant of the ram he slew years before. Freed of the need for and fear of ultimate consummation, he can with Anastasia "sweetly" nap and play and rest "content" (742–43). Having found that all distinctions, including those between "Sense and Nonsense," "Futility and Purpose," and "Same and Different," no longer hold any meaning for him, he now accepts "without much grumble" all "the ineluctable shortcomings of mortal studenthood" (755–56). "[E]mpowered as it were by impotence, driven by want of motive" (756), and aided by the goat with whom he has reestablished an affinity, he seemingly is capable of driving out his rival, the protean "false" "Grand Tutor," Harold Bray.

By passing through paradox to see that any proposition is "as misleading" and therefore "as satisfactory" as any other (759), George perhaps frees himself internally from the logic of "Grand-Tutorhood," but in the less enlightened eyes of his society he is still bound by it,

still committed to deliver the promise implicit in his choice of name
and course. Since he believes that what he has or has not learned cannot be transmitted, he is incapable of fulfilling the communal function of the "invested one" who, according to Campbell, traditionally
gains through initiation the competence "to enact himself the role of
the initiator."[22] "Freedom" and "Bondage" may be "finally undiffer-
entiable" (759), but, unable to complete the full mythological round
and bestow the hero's boon, deliver "the Answer" and studentdom,
he is bound, like Bray, to be cast out. In projecting the conclusion
of his life-story in the "Posttape," he thus incorporates the basic pattern of tragic fiction, the tendency to isolate the hero from his society.[23]

Moreover, the truth George embraced in the "Belly" is "unspeakable" not simply because the gospel cannot be communicated but also
because it is "bad news." Having given up the "utter freedom" of
innocence to discover the liberating "Answer" and know "what must
be done" (732), he learns that the price one must pay is time. Completing his fall into self-knowledge, he, like Adam, "enters his own
created life" and is conscious of his subjection to "the order of nature
as we know it." As Frye argues, "Aristotle's hamartia" is "a condition
of being, not a cause of becoming," for when Adam falls, "he enters
a world in which existence is itself tragic, not existence modified by
an act, deliberate or unconscious. Merely to exist is to disturb the
balance of nature. . . . This fact, in itself ironic and now called
Angst, becomes tragic when a sense of a lost and originally higher destiny is added to it."[24]

Earlier in the narrative, George had related his reaction to a performance of *The Tragedy of Taliped Decanus*, a parodic "modern translation" (312) of *Oedipus the King*, containing some of "the touchingest
words and music" he has ever heard (346). What he finds particularly
moving is "the *kommos*, or *lament*," which concludes with the "committee" (chorus) singing a series of rhetorical questions:

> *Why did you murder your daddy, my friend?*
> *Why did you roger your mommy? And*
> *Why must we sing this refrain again?*
> *Boo hoo hoo.*

(346)

Like Sophocles' tragic ruler, Barth's burlesque hero, Taliped, learns
that he has been condemned to follow a preordained pattern, a course

prefigured in prophecy and predetermined by natural law. The solution Oedipus arrives at is "man," mortal and overreaching; the one Taliped offers is "Mother Campus" (Mother Nature), the *"mother"* that *"eats up all her children"* (322). Discovering that ontogeny does indeed recapitulate phylogeny, both gain the knowledge that they cannot refrain from repeating the refrain.

Assuming there is no ultimate "Answer" to the "committee"'s "Why?" are we to view such recycling as Futility or Purpose? Looked at from the divinely comic perspective of Campbell's mythic hero who has completely and joyfully accepted his role in the cosmic round, recurrence is the continuous revalidation of "the majesty of Being," but from the perspective of the isolated individual who is incapable of coping so easily with the "bad news" that he is mortal, the validation of "the Law of Cyclology" may be cause for something other than rejoicing. George's response in the "Posttape" is "No matter"; the question is pointless, for "Futility and Purpose" are meaningless concepts. Nevertheless, as the bliss of "Being" gives way to what Barth has termed "the spirit of *post coitum triste*"[25] and the text proffers allusions to *Oedipus at Colonus*, the Goat-Boy's final comments reveal an increasing preoccupation with temporality and limitation. History and his recorded story may consist of "cycles on cycles," but his "self-wound watch runs fast" (755), and in terms of the individual human life, there is no way of rewinding "the very tape of time" (742). Knowing now that he, like Max, "exists," he considers the possible implications of reversing the proposition that "ontogeny recapitulates cosmogeny," suggests that because there "is an entropy to time" and "the pans" must ultimately become imbalanced for the worse (763), not only his case but "everything that is the case" may be diagnosed as terminal.

Since George's final stance in a way incorporates the tragicomic nihilism of Todd Andrews and Jacob Horner (his "No matter," for example, exactly echoing one of Todd's last statements), and since his fall and Eben's are in a manner similar, by the time we reach the "Posttape" it has become clear that in *Giles* Barth is imitating his own canon, reintroducing themes and voices from the earlier works into the contrapuntal composition that is his "Revised New Syllabus." This, along with the apparent links between the Goat-Boy's life story and J. B.'s, may lead us to view George's ultimate stance as commenting on the satirist's own, particularly if we recall that what the "committee" in *Taliped Decanus* laments is not only the mock-hero's fate, but also the realization that they themselves are bound to repeat "the refrain again."

In a perceptive essay exploring the fusion of tragedy and satire in *Giles* and the relationship between the work and the attitude of Menippean satire, James Gresham has pointed out that most Menippean satires "reflect ambivalence toward Romance, toward the Real, and toward lucidity" and that "[s]atiric attack on the Ideal (or Romance) can at least potentially shift to satyric celebration of the Real—with tragic overtones."[26] To move just a step beyond this is to find in the tragic elements of the Goat-Boy's tale a suggestion of tragic overtones to the paradoxical position implicit in all four of the books by Barth discussed so far. For if the satirist is constrained by his own self-consciousness, by his historical sense or sense of audience, to write burlesques and parodies, or if, in order to affirm his own creative detachment, he is compelled to keep reminding us that he is presenting not "revelations" but his own "mad dreams," he must confront the fact that he has by necessity or choice relinquished the role of spokesman of his society articulating latent or requisite poetic thought, or must face the possibility that that way lies solipsism. If his rejection of abstractions, systems, and the Ideal, his desire for lucidity, induce him to focus on the Real, on the facts of life, at the end of that road waits the "bad news" that existence itself is tragic. He may invite us to lose ourselves with him for a time in his weirdly logical fantasies, in the arbitrary complexity of his fictional cycles within cycles, to share in his apparent victory over common sense, but lurking somewhere is the knowledge that reading, like ontogeny, is finally linear.

Some may find, then, that by alluding to the plight of the parodist, Barth has escalated travesty to "something more passionate," that by emphasizing George's isolation and mortality while effecting what seems to be a shift in tone in the "Posttape," he has not only reorchestrated the pattern but regenerated some of the emotion of tragedy. We cannot forget, however, that the Goat-Boy's "University" is informed by a tendency to counter both emotions and motions, that in this composition, the voice that makes a point may be only a part of the counterpoint. The "committee" bemoans having to sing the refrain again, and J. B. is disturbed by the tone of his Grand-Tutor's last words, but the text displays the satirist's verbal exuberance, the satyr's celebration of physicality, and its author, like Bray, pulls a disappearing act, assuming and discarding masks and escaping through the cracks in and between the frames. Although

George's story imitates the tragedy named *Oedipus the King*, it also imitates the travesty called *Taliped Decanus*. Furthermore, the remarks he makes "in the spirit of *post coitum triste*" are preceded by a description of fulfillment through consummation and undercut by the demonstration of the document's spuriousness that follows them, and even as he is resigning himself to "Fate," he reminds us that all he and we have experienced may be but the "ironic" details of "a mad collective dream" (756). While it may be true, as Frye suggests, that, even though Joyce's mythic hero never wakes up, when we have finished *Finnegans Wake* "it dawns on us that it is the *reader* who achieves the quest," when we complete Barth's own "encyclopaedic" work what we have learned is what we are told at the end of Williams's *Paterson*, that all we can know is

> the dance, to dance to a measure
> contrapuntally,
>   Satyrically, the tragic foot.[27]

Chapter Six

"Water-Message":

If a significant segment of the reading public has come to associate Barth's name with innovation, experimentation, and exhaustion, his fiction with self-reference and self-indulgence, this reputation is based to a large extent on the two books that appeared in the decade following the publication of *Giles Goat-Boy*. Timing seems to have had a great deal to do with this, for *Lost in the Funhouse* and *Chimera* were issued in a period during which a number of factors conjoined to insure that the works would become both highly visible and susceptible to a certain kind of interpretation. *The Sot-Weed Factor* had earned Barth a fair amount of critical attention and something akin to a cult following, *Giles Goat-Boy* had won him a much wider audience, and revised editions of his first three books had been published by Doubleday in 1967, generating a new wave of reviews. Moreover, by the late 1960s and early 1970s, developments in literary criticism had begun to catch up with developments in contemporary fiction, the rapid proliferation of critical studies on earlier authors had encouraged growing numbers of scholars to focus on the work of contemporary writers, and the popularization of the ideas of Marshall McLuhan had created an atmosphere conducive to an acceptance of the "intermedia" experimentation of *Lost in the Funhouse*. Finally, even if many of them, as Barth claims, widely misinterpreted it, a good number of readers took his essay on Borges as a prologemena to any future fiction, linked "The Literature of Exhaustion" with the stories and novellas Barth produced in the same period, and came to view the latter, therefore, as representing the clearest and most definitive embodiments of his aesthetic and metaphysics.

While the validity and usefulness of such valuations are debatable, what is more certain is that *Lost in the Funhouse* and *Chimera* are integral parts of the continuum that is Barth's oeuvre. The former, for instance, continues, and perhaps in a way completes and reverses ("Unwind, rewind, replay"), the retrograde recapitulation of the evolution of the species Homo poeticus that characterizes the development of Barth's earlier fiction. Having previously parodied realism, reorchestrated some of the conventions of the eighteenth-century novel, and created a comic Old Testament, in *Lost in the Funhouse* he seemingly brings not only the novel but literature itself full circle by taking us back "to the oral tradition out of which literature comes."[1] Whether it is interpreted as an authorial pretense or a statement of authorial intention, the "Author's Note" to the volume indicates that many of its "members" are meant for "recorded authorial voice," or "live authorial voice," "live or recorded voices," or to be "read as if heard so."[2] "Dunyazadiad" in *Chimera*, of course, reaches back through the tradition in a different way, playing upon one of the most famous oral storytelling situations recorded in literature.

Barth's "Fiction for Print, Tape, Live Voice" (the subtitle of *Lost in the Funhouse*), moreover, is just as progressive as regressive, for in "exploring the possibilities" opened up by the use of tapes he is suggesting that one may escape literary exhaustion not only by "investigating roots" but also by employing the fruits of modern technology. Exploiting the potential of the electronic medium, he has indicated, is "a way of having it both ways." On the one hand, you "have the authorial voice, after all, telling the stories when you work on tape. On the other hand, unlike purely oral literature, a tape has some of the virtues of print: it's interruptable and referable. You can stop a tape, as you can't stop a live storyteller, and you can go back to a particular point—two things that you *can* do on the page that you can't do in the movie theatre, for example, and that you couldn't do with the live oral tradition very easily." Like this experimentation with the means of presentation, the use of myth in both *Lost in the Funhouse* and *Chimera* also represents a kind of progressive regression. Whereas *The Sot-Weed Factor* and *Giles Goat-Boy* are informed by the pattern of the "monomyth" and replete with allusions to mythological figures and situations, in composing many of the pieces in the two later volumes Barth decided to reject the "mythopoeically retrograde" approach of writing "about our daily experiences in order to point up to the myths," choosing instead "to address" the "mythic archetypes" more "directly."[3]

Although the two books are linked to and advance Barth's earlier work in numerous other ways, such as the facts that both play a great number of new variations on the triangle and on the principle that ontogeny recapitulates phylogeny, what is perhaps most apparent to the reader is the seemingly more blatant emphasis on resonance and increased preoccupation with "the secret adventures of order." One of the "Seven Additional Author's Notes" that appear in the Bantam edition of *Lost in the Funhouse*, for instance, states that the "regnant idea" behind the author's indicating "ideal media" of "presentation" is "the unpretentious one of turning as many aspects of the fiction as possible—the structure, the narrative viewpoint, the means of presentation, in some instances the process of composition and/or recitation as well as of reading or listening—into dramatically relevant emblems of the theme" (x). Its fourteen pieces, the author tells us, "are meant to be received 'all at once' " and to be perceived as constituting "neither a collection nor a selection, but a series" (ix). The first of them is an emblematic "Frame-Tale," and many play with such patterns as the "regressus in infinitum" (114). The title of *Chimera* emblemizes its nature as "a kind of monstrous mixed metaphor."[4] Here Chinese boxes again abound, and the fictional universe appears to be governed by the principles of numerology. One of its constituent parts, "Perseid," exhibits a "complicated structure" that is based upon "the Fibonacci series of numbers as it manifests itself in the logarithmic spiral" and that Barth himself once termed "almost, but not quite, completely arbitrary."[5]

A Moebius Strip

Whereas the geometry of "Perseid" is spiral, the structure of *Lost in the Funhouse*, we are led to believe, is a closed loop. Its "Frame-Tale" is a kit for constructing a Moebius strip which the reader is free to regard as "one-, two-, or three-dimensional" (ix). Once it is completed mentally or physically, the loop becomes an emblem of the "Law of Cyclology" and all its corollaries, including the propositions that make up the "monomyth." As a continuous tape, it not only reminds us of the Grand Tutor's "endless tapes" but also suggests the means of presentation of many of the pieces in the book, and it is thus emblematic of Barth's recycling of elements of his own fictions and of the oral-literary tradition. This connection with the tradition is further reinforced by the nature of the message that is both conveyed by and inscribed on the "Frame-Tale." For in joining headpiece to tailpiece, the reader helps to bring into being a story that reads "ONCE UPON A TIME THERE WAS A STORY THAT BEGAN ONCE UPON A TIME . . ." (ad infinitum), serves as midwife at the birth of a headless, tailless, and at least theoretically endless tale that may have been conceived as a result of Barth's love affair with Scheherazade.

As a participant in a panel discussion that took place in March of 1975, Barth talked about the ramifications of a typographical error in "Perseid," stated that he does not know what he has "written when" he has "written a book," and went on to add the following remarks:

> My hair was raised (that's a metaphor) when I was doing some homework in *The Thousand and One Nights* for a piece I was writing, and I realized the formula in the Arabic . . . for beginning a story like *The Thousand and One Nights*, after the invocation to Allah, is the following: "There is a book called *The Thousand and One Nights* in which it is written that there was this king Shahryar, this vizier, and his daughter Scheherazade," and the rest. Now we're reading it, and on the page it says: "There is a book called *The Thousand and One Nights* in which it is said. . . ." Where is that book? At that moment I realized that while I thought I was an Aristotelian, I am in fact a Platonist, and that all novelists are practicing Platonists. Because if that book exists anywhere, it is in the heaven of ideas.[6]

If such comments lead us to interpret "Frame-Tale" as indicating that the book is but a copy of the Book, what Barth says elsewhere may lead us to interpret it as suggesting that the book is also one that copies itself. In "The Literature of Exhaustion" he points out that one of Borges's "frequenter literary allusions is to the 602nd night of *The 1001 Nights*, when, owing to a copyist's error, Scheherazade begins to tell the story of the 1001 nights, from the beginning. Happily, the King interrupts; if he didn't there'd be no 603rd night ever, and while this would solve Scheherazade's problem—which is every story-teller's problem: to publish or perish—it would put the 'outside' author in a bind." The Argentine artificer who, as Barth suspects, "dreamed this whole thing up," himself states the "now infinite and circular" story embraces itself "monstrously," its reiteration representing a "curious danger" to the "transfixed" auditor.[7] What both Barth and Borges find "hair-raising" are the ontological questions raised. "Why does it make us uneasy," Borges asks, to know that "the thousand and one nights are within the book of *A Thousand and One Nights*?" The answer, he proposes, is that such "inversions suggest that if the characters in a story can be readers or spectators, then we, their readers or spectators, can be fictitious. In 1833 Carlyle observed that universal history is an infinite sacred book that all men write and read and try to understand, and in which they too are written."[8]

It is these troubling ontological implications that add the twist to Barth's "Frame-Tale," alerting us to the presence in *Lost in the Funhouse* of the phenomenon Douglas R. Hofstadter has labeled "Strange Loopiness." In his fascinating, Pulitzer Prize–winning work *Gödel, Escher, Bach: An Eternal Golden Braid*, Hofstadter indicates that the " 'Strange Loop' phenomenon occurs whenever, by moving upwards (or downwards) through the levels of some hierarchical system, we can unexpectedly find ourselves right back where we started." Although Hofstadter examines many "Tangled Hierarchies," or systems "in which a Strange Loop occurs," the one most nearly analogous to *Lost in the Funhouse* is the world of M. C. Escher, the Dutch graphic artist who was himself enamored of the Moebius strip:

In some of his drawings, one single theme can appear on different levels of reality. For instance, one level in a drawing might clearly be recognizable as representing fantasy or imagination; another level would be recognizable as reality. These two levels might be the only explicitly portrayed levels. But the mere presence of these two levels invites the viewer to look upon himself as part of yet another level; and by taking that step, the viewer cannot help getting caught up in Escher's implied chain of levels, in which, for any one level, there is always another level above it of greater "reality," and likewise, there is always a level below "more imaginary" than it is. This can be mind-boggling in itself. However, what happens if the chain of levels is not linear, but forms a loop? What is real, then, and what is fantasy?[9]

Implicit in the "Tangled Hierarchies" of Escher's drawings or Borges' "story-within-the-story turned back upon itself" or Barth's "Frame-Tale" is a basic conflict between the finite and the infinite that gives rise to "a strong sense of paradox,"[10] and this is something else that links *Lost in the Funhouse* to Barth's earlier fiction, for, as we have seen, the exposure of the inherent paradoxes in hierarchical systems has always been a useful strategem for him to employ, serving both as a means of creating aesthetic resolution and as an expression of his satiric attitude.

Constituting a "Strange Loop" that bears an affinity to Scheherazade's six hundred and second tale, "Frame-Tale" serves, then, as an invitation to lose ourselves in an ontologically perplexing funhouse where distortions of distortions generate finite representations of the infinite and the first and last members of Barth's "series" appear to link up, turning the terminal into the perpetual, the linear into the cyclical. The existence of the "Funhouse," of course, requires the interaction "of three terms—teller, tale, told—each dependent on the other two but not in the same ways" ("Life-Story," 118), and while it offers the possibility of substituting "almost death" for death, its closed loops and infinite regressions threaten, like Scheherazade's ploy, to put not only the "outside" author but the reader/auditor "in a bind." For if Scheherazade is permitted to persist, if "Frame-Tale" is permitted to continue along its recursive course, there can be no six hundred and third night ever, Barth's story can never really begin, and to be put in the position of Shahryar, to have one's desire for completeness and consummation perpetually frustrated, may be a less than satisfying experience. By placing his Moebius strip in our hands, where we may turn it until our own exhaustion takes over, Barth may be acknowledging both the necessity of our participation and the limits to our sufferance. Moreover, just as one must ignore the trompe l'oeil in an Escher drawing in order to get caught up in a chain of levels, so too must we avoid noticing that Barth's closed loop is a feat of legerdemain if we are to remain "fixed" and continue repeating the refrain. Handling it according to his instructions, we may find that the illusion has been quickly dispelled, that our attention has almost inevitably been drawn to the Real, to pulp and ink. Discovering that the strip is not multi- but merely three-dimensional, we may also be led to discover the inviolate level that exists below every tangled hierarchy.[11]

Lost in the Funhouse

To become convinced that "Frame-Tale" is indeed emblematic of the "Funhouse" as a whole, one need only move on to the first piece in the series proper, for "Night-Sea Journey" is marked by recycling, depends on a bit of gimmickry, and invites the reader to become enmeshed in a tangle of physical and metaphysical hierarchies. The narrator who both swims in and generates this ocean of story is a spermatozoon, "tale-bearer of a generation" (9). Ontogeny here is the recapitulation of ontology, and "the Heritage" (4) transported is not only genetic but literary and mythic. Barth's choice of narrator is yet another thing that links his work with Sterne's, for in recounting the circumstances of his conception, Tristram Shandy refers to the general sixteenth- and seventeenth-century belief that each spermatozoon contains a homunculus, a little man "as much and as truly our fellow-creature as my Lord Chancellor of England." Speaking of the dangers his "little gentleman" must have faced in his solitary travels, Tristram wonders what might have happened had he "got to his journey's end miserably spent" and "in this sad disorder'd state of nerves . . . laid down a prey to sudden starts, or a series of melancholy dreams and fancies. . . ."[12] Similarly, Barth's own homunculus is "exhausted and dispirited," wonders whether he has lost his senses, and indicates that he too is "vulnerable to dreams" (3, 9). Unlike Sterne's minute voyager, however, Barth's swimmer raves to himself (10); believing that he is "the sole survivor" of a "fell journey" (9), that, like Melville's Ishmael, he "Only" has "escaped alone to tell" (Job 1:14–19), he howls of the loss of "the best swimmers of" his "generation" (4) and questions Job-like the nature and design of his "Maker," the purpose of his trial.

In considering the possibility that he may be a "Hero" and in referring to his trial as a "night-sea journey," the "tale-bearer" engages in a bit of mythopoetizing, defines his absurd swim as the archetypal voyage of the sun, the passage through the earth womb or in the belly of the whale, the descent into the underworld that begins with an entry into a labyrinth or spiral.[13] The maze he has entered is both anatomical and speculative, for as he is drawn inexorably "Herward" (9), he engages in a series of "eschatological" musings that in jest "perhaps illumine certain speculations of Lord Raglan, Carl Jung, and Joseph Campbell" (x), while seeming to illustrate in utero the truth of one of Borges's favorite Platonic utterances: "It is an arduous task to discover the maker and father of this universe, and, after discovering him, it is impossible to declare him to all men."[14] Just as Plato offers us in dialogue the words of Socrates and Timaeus, Barth's brooder conveys the conjectures of one of his "late companions," including such tangled hierarchies as a universe in which "Makers and swimmers *each generate the other*," or one consisting of "cycles within cycles, either finite or infinite" where "the 'night-sea,' as it were, in which Makers 'swam' and created nightseas and swimmers like ourselves, might be the creation of a larger Maker, Himself one of many, Who in turn et cetera" (8). Like his biblical forebear, however, this garrulous gamete "multiplieth words without knowledge" (Job 35:16). Talking to himself, "to keep" his "reason in" the "awful darkness" (10), he finds that such "recesses from swimming" are what "sustain" him "in the swim" but must acknowledge that the purpose of his journey is ultimately unspeakable; even when mythologized it can be described only in the same abstractions that fail to define the goal of the Goat-Boy's quest: *"consummation, transfiguration, union of contraries, transcension of categories"* (3, 10).

Reciting his companion's hypotheses, he temporarily loses and finds himself in eddies of reflection, his words drowning out for a time the call of selfless "Love," the name we give to "our ignorance of what whips us," what draws us toward a paradoxical consummation that is "the death of us, yet our salvation and resurrection; simultaneously our journey's end, mid-point, and commencement" (4, 10). "Rehearsing" (3; pun surely intended) many of the stances assumed by Barth's earlier imaginative progeny, he attempts to identify himself as an "utterest nay-sayer," as *"he who abjures and rejects the night-sea journey"* (12, 11). Yet, even though he tries to resist, though he hopes to convince his unseen auditor, the being he will become, to stop his hearing against the siren's song and "Make no more," he is compelled to join in repeating the refrain: "Love! Love! Love!" (12). In true Menippean fashion, his speculations buy him time but account for nothing, and if we are cognizant of his "actual nature" and realize that his words are "merely correct" (x), the labyrinth of abstraction becomes transparent, revealing the machinery of natural law, and the tide of the speaker's vagrant prose becomes synonymous with the tragicomic ebb and flow of the Real.

Mythic pretensions, water symbolism, and the extended use of the phylogenetic conceit link "Night-Sea Journey" with "Ambrose His Mark," the first of three stories in the series explicitly about the would-be "Maker" Ambrose M ____ (Mensch). While it may be true that it was a colleague who suggested he use "Ambrose," Barth could hardly have settled on a more resonant Christian name for his nascent artist-hero.[15] Not only is it associated with lucidity and illumination (the Ambrose Lightship), hallucination and immortality (ambrosia), but also, via St. Ambrose, with the Word and the Book. A fourth-century bishop of Milan, Ambrose is known for having possessed great oratorical power, composed magnificent hymns, and introduced antiphonal singing and the use of neumes to represent musical notes. Perhaps most significant, he was, Augustine tells us, the first person to read silently, beginning what Borges refers to as "the mental process" that "would culminate, after many centuries, in the predominance of the written word over the spoken one, of the pen over the voice," initiating the "strange art" that "would lead, many years later, to the concept of the book as an end in itself, not as a means to an end."[16]

As mock myth, "Ambrose His Mark" begins anew the night-sea journey, revealing the unusual aspects of the archetypal hero's birth and the sign of his vocation, recording the seemingly portentous circumstances surrounding his naming. The spermatozoon may have called for an end to making, to the " 'immortality-chain,' " the "cyclic process of incarnation" (8), but if he has generated Ambrose and the tale he bears, flesh and word have been made again. Furthermore, since the "Law of Cyclology" seems to be operant, the apparently synchronous patterns of bildungsroman, *Künstlerroman*, and romance begin to reemerge, if only through parody, as both hero and text develop along generic lines and struggle to make "Sense" (12).

In recalling the eighteenth chapter of *Moby-Dick* ("His Mark"), the title of this first chapter of Ambrose's history suggests that *his* mark, like Queequeg's, is not only a significant sign expressing his secret name, nature, and destiny but also a signature left by his Maker, a key to the mysterious plan that makes sense of both ontogeny and cosmology. When Melville's heathen enrolls among the Pequod's company, he signs his name by making "an exact counterpart of a queer round figure" that is "tattooed upon his arm," one of the many "hieroglyphic marks" written on his body by "a departed prophet and seer" and constituting "a complete theory of the heavens and the earth, and a mystical treatise on the art of attaining truth." Thus, Ishmael tells us, "Queequeg in his own proper person was a riddle to unfold; a wondrous work in one volume" revealing the mysteries not of any particular sect, but the universal truths disclosed to those cosmophilists who have been initiated into "the great and everlasting First Congregation of this whole worshipping world."[17]

Just as Queequeg must bear the misnomers "Quohog" and "Hedgehog," so too must Ambrose respond to *"Honig"* and even "Christine" until a "naming-sign" (30), an extraordinary swarming of bees about the birthmark on his face, leads his relations to name him after the saint who as a child allegedly shared a similar experience. The occurrence seems auspicious since, as Uncle Konrad notes, the swarm of bees that settled on the mouth of Ambrose's namesake was interpreted as an omen indicating that "he'd grow up to be a great speaker" (31). Moreover, the descriptions of a baptismal service being enacted nearby, the etymology of his name itself, and the mythic association of bees and honey with "Her" milk, with the maternal water of life, all appear to mark Ambrose as not only a potential master of words but as a bringer of the Word, an artist-hero capable of completing the night-sea journey to gain immortality by discovering and transmitting the secrets of the Great Mother.

The narrative mode of the story, however, is first-person usual; the tone Ambrose employs in telling his tale is, if anything, *mock*-heroic; and the points of congruence between his account of his birth and naming and Tristram Shandy's own recollection of those significant events may cause one to wonder whether all this "ado" (25) is about nothing, whether Uncle Konrad's notions about the importance of portents have as much relevance as Walter Shandy's theories about names and noses. Both Queequeg's hieroglyphic tattoos and Ambrose's mark may connote gnosis, but the harpooneer cannot "read" the "mysteries" inscribed on his "living parchment"[18] and Ambrose's birthmark is "ambiguous" (32). To "Aunt Rosa" "its three lobes" resemble "the wings and abdomen of a bee in flight," yet she may be misconstrued as calling it a *B* (" 'Oh boy,' Konrad sighed. 'Nah, it is a bee! A regular bee! I declare' "), and if it looks like a "purple bee" flying "upside down without benefit of head," it also looks like those anatomical features that make "the *Honig*" an Ambrose and not a Christine (29–30). (*B*, of course, is indeed the signature of his Maker, the jester who has a good deal of fun in the story with double entendres involving drones and stingers.)

Our hero himself notes that it "was to be" his "fate to wonder at that moniker, relish and revile it, ignore it, stare it out of countenance into hieroglyph and gibber," knowing full well that he and his "sign are neither one nor quite two" (32). His use of "moniker" is apt, for it is a term in which the single sign has doubled (monogram and marker), emblemizing his remarks about the duplicity of language, remarks reminiscent of Jacob Horner's own comments about the inaccuracy of words, the necessary distortion involved in assigning names to things. If all the signposts lend themselves to misinterpretation, if the hieroglyphs are ambiguous, then the way through the labyrinth is not clearly marked and Ambrose cannot accurately translate the book of himself. Even if the swarming of bees on his eyes and ears may be taken as a sign that "he'll grow up to see things clear" and not as an indication that he will be blinded by Oedipal innocence, will be stung by or stop his "hearing against Her song" ("Night-Sea Journey," 12), the bees do not light on his mouth as they did on the saint's, and there is nothing to foretoken that his vision will be anything but "unspeakable." Rather than returning him to the font, the womb of guiding "Grace" (25), Ambrose's unorthodox baptism results in his being "weaned not only from" his mother's "milk but from her care" (29). His birthmark, thus, becomes also the mark of his solitude and exile, the mark of Cain. It would be years, he tells us, "before anyone troubled" to complete his "birth certificate, whereon" his "surname was preceded by a blank" (32), a blank he must in a sense fill in himself, perhaps like that other *B*, Henry Burlingame, by asserting, choosing "his gods and devils on the run," and quilling "his own name upon the universe."

The concept that, as Borges puts it, "universal history" is a "Sacred Scripture" we "decipher and write uncertainly," or that "we are the versicles or words or letters of a magic book,"[19] is one of the basic conceits Barth toys with in *Lost in the Funhouse*, and it is again predominant in the second Ambrose story in the series. Corresponding to the stage in the hero's journey known as "the call to adventure," "Water-Message" once more confronts the would-be reader of signs with a blankness. Here and in the title story, water imagery carries us not only to the womb-font and Clio's spring, but also to Actaeon's stream, Narcissus's pool, and the Abyss.

Remaining close to Ambrose's point of view and employing a tone that tempers mild mockery with indulgence, a narrator takes us through his subject's preadolescent awakening to *"Nature's Secrets"* (43). Comic allusions indicate that, in this context at least, the "monomyth" is to be interpreted as an elaborate metaphor for the innocent's initiation into the mundane secrets of Mars and Venus. "Scylla and Charybdis," for example, is the name Ambrose gives to a particularly dangerous part of his route home from school, a place where he must navigate between a vicious "Spitz dog" and "Crazy Alice" (39), and where he one day encounters the belligerent Wimpy James. Escaping this ogre by "playing the clown," and feeling that he is therefore "No man at all," he recoups by imagining himself as "Odysseus steering under anvil clouds" or a Herculean hero borne "aloft to the stars" (41–44).

Ignorant of and insecure about the "facts of life" (40), Ambrose creates fictions in which he performs heroically in worlds that are not the case. Too young to be initiated into "the Occult Order of the Sphinx" and share the sexual knowledge of older boys such as his appropriately named sibling, Peter, he hopes that mastery of the word will be the key to the mysteries of the flesh, pores over *The Book of*

Knowledge, turns over names and phrases as if they were magical, transformative. When he discovers a note in a bottle, therefore, he believes that "the word" has "wandered willy-nilly to his threshold," illuminating not only the rites conducted in the older boys' "Den" at the heart of the "voluptuous" and mysterious "labyrinth" called "the Jungle," but also a "greater vision, vague and splendrous, whereof the sea-wreathed bottle" is "an emblem" (46, 52). If we forge a connection between this "water message" and Barth's spermatozoon, who is also both "vessel and contents" (3), then we may share in Ambrose's anticipation, expect him to receive phylogenetic knowledge and the Great Mother's guidance. Indeed, the narrator leads us on, describing the paper the message is written on in language ("tablet," "thrice," 53), subtly suggestive of hermetic wisdom.

Like those other "Saints," Eben and George, however, Ambrose finds that the world refuses to meet his expectations, for this MS. found in a bottle consists only of a general salutation—"TO WHOM IT MAY CONCERN"—and a complimentary close—"YOURS TRULY" (53). The rest is a blank, and, noticing that "those shiny bits in the paper's texture" are "splinters of wood pulp" (54), he has his attention drawn to the Real, just as ours is if we look closely at the book's "Frame-Tale." The demystifying message the sea sends is that it may be taken as a void, an emblem of the world's arbitrariness and finality, of the cruel and seductive call of Love, or a surface in which one may see his reflection, stare at his moniker, and fill in the blank with and by himself. The only apparent alternative to joining in singing "Her" senseless song is to answer "Ambrose, Ambrose, Ambrose, Ambrose!" ("Ambrose His Mark," 32).

These alternatives are more elaborately emblemized in the title story of the series, one of the most widely known and frequently critiqued of Barth's works, and the last of the three pieces focusing on Ambrose per se (three for the trinity, Hermes Trismegistus, the lobes of his mark, etc.). By the time we reach this spot on the loop, ontogeny has progressed to the point of pubescence, the mythic quest to the stage of the hero's trials in the bowels of the labyrinth. The figure who presides over adolescent Ambrose's adventures in the Ocean City funhouse is "Fat May the Laughing Lady," a steatopygous Venus, mechanical Great Mother, whose amplified chuckles, groans, and tears may be a response to the comic absurdity of the night-sea journey or to his efforts to escape it by playing the clown. Having become painfully aware of the enticements of Magda, a well-developed companion, whose name designates her as an avatar of the archetypal Virgin-Whore, Ambrose enters "Her" domain. Unable to find his bearings in this frowzy and fantastic kingdom by the sea, he, like the "tale-bearer," is at best ambivalent about the groping passage through "Love's Tunnel's fearsome obstacles" (77). The funhouse may be fun for lovers or cosmophilists, but for "Ambrose it is *a place of fear and confusion*" (69) where something inexplicable whips us, generation after generation, to engage in mechanical multiplication, where "Her" song is the "shluppish whisper, continuous as seawash round the globe," that "tidelike falls and rises with the circuit of dawn and dusk" (76–77). Confronting the facts of life in the funhouse-world, he finds that any view of it is a distortion, "that *nothing*" is "what it" looks "like," each person a fabricator who practices "mythotherapy" and views "himself as the hero of the story" (87).

He realizes, moreover, that in "the funhouse mirror-room you can't see yourself go on forever, because no matter how you stand, your head gets in the way" (81–82)—self-consciousness makes one aware of the inviolate level that enables the illusion of a tangled hierarchy to come into existence; self-awareness makes one conscious that what the mirror sees is funny and that "She" offers but a "poor sort of immortality" ("Night-Sea Journey," 10). In contrast to the presumably less (self)-conscious Peter and Magda, who find "the right exit" and go "all the way, through," (82, 77), Ambrose falls prey to Barth's "metaphysical emotion," is led by ontological speculation into a "Strange Loop," a spiral part of the funhouse "that winds around on itself like a whelk shell" (80). The "simple, radical difference about him," either "genius" or "madness," makes it impossible for him simply to "*be*" (85, 79), to accept unconsciously and satyrically the arbitrariness and finality of a natural order in which "millions of living animals devoured one another" (87), even though he knows that "the world" is "*going on*," that the "town, the river, himself," are "not imaginary" and time is real (85). He wishes he could end his "life absolutely without pain" (86), but he cannot. He finds a "name-coin" that may be "suggestive" of lucidity and immortality as well as "the famous lightship" and "his late grandfather's favorite dessert" (90), but, like George's assignment, it belongs or belonged to someone else, and he encounters no signs that can be simply translated to reveal the maze's "secret" (85). He and we may imagine alternative "possible endings" characterized by heroic struggles, miraculous rescues and escapes, or the revelation of the "funhouse operator" (83–

84), but such "stories" told oneself "in the dark" (92) have a tendency to degenerate from romance to cliché. Having "strayed into" this "pass *wherein he lingers yet*," Ambrose cannot pass and may even "have ceased to search" for the "way" (91–92). And so, though it will not alter his loneliness or the likelihood that he will die talking to himself to keep his reason, "though he would rather be among the lovers," he decides as consolation to "construct funhouses for others and be their secret operator" (94). If it is difficult for him to be one kind of Maker he will try his hand at becoming another; if he is unable to interpret and voice the book that is world or self, he will try to design one that is an end in itself.

In the reading, of course, "Lost in the Funhouse" is a good deal less solemn and straightforward than the preceding summary would indicate. The narrator himself plays the clown, lacing his language with puns, pointing to pregnant passages, and burlesquing his role and ours through the use of "heavy-footed" symbolism (90), particularly of the Freudian and Jungian sorts. His labored and labyrinthine narrative gets sidetracked, backtracks, and diverges, explores numerous culs-de-sac. When we are told that Ambrose "fell into" the "habit of rehearsing to himself the unadventurous story of his life, narrated from the third-person point of view" (92), we are threatened with Scheherazade's monstrous tale. When we learn of his decision to become an artificer, we are being invited to help create and lose ourselves in an infinite regression, a hall of mirrors in which A, a constructor of funhouses, exists in a funhouse constructed by B, who exists. . . .

Much of the narrative ado in the story consists of the exposure of the limits and artifices of literary realism, and of the narrator's infertility, aesthetic and technical faux pas, and false starts, his inability to complete his inquiry. Like dilapidated Ocean City, the house that James built would appear to be decrepit, "worn out" (85), and the uninspired narrator seems incapable of completing the passage, laments the fact that he may be repeating a tired and tiresome refrain. There have been readers who, interpreting such devices and comments as authorial statements, have concluded that Barth believes that the possibilities of fiction have been exhausted and that he has been reduced to making the most of what some of them find to be an annoyingly self-indulgent brand of self-consciousness. Not only is it true that the same things could conceivably be said of Sterne, but also that this kind of response fails to do justice to Barth's use of "the narrative viewpoint" and "the process of composition" as "dramatically relevant emblems" (x).

For one thing, the way in which Barth plays the role of author in the tale helps to create the aforementioned chain of levels of reality, fostering the illusion that in this fiction it may be possible to "go on forever," suggesting the type of *regressus in infinitum* that, according to Borges, may be used to convince oneself that "what all idealists admit" is correct—"the world is hallucinatory."[20] At the same time, however, by showing his hand, "the author . . . of this story" almost inevitably reminds us of the existence of a very mortal Maker who has constructed a funhouse out of perishable ink and paper and who owes that existence to the fact that "in approximately the year when Lord Baltimore was granted charter to the province of Maryland by Charles I, five hundred twelve women . . . received into themselves the intromittent organs of five hundred twelve men" (76). The effect is much the same as that produced by the Escher lithograph "Drawing Hands" in which a pair of hands appear to arise out of a picture within the picture and draw each other as well as the picture of which they are, and are not, a part. Just as "Lost in the Funhouse" puts a tangle in the hierarchy consisting of teller and tale, Escher's piece twists together the hierarchical levels of drawer and drawn while also calling attention to the process of composition and, therefore, to the undrawn hands of the artist and the invisible inviolate level where, from one point of view, the "immortality chain" can "terminate" ("Night-Sea Journey," 8).[21] Both works of art interweave the mundane and the mad dream and display an apparent conflict between the finite and the infinite, but Barth's "Funhouse" evokes an especially strong sense of paradox arising out of a conflict between the Real and the Ideal. The very ordinariness of Ambrose's "difference," the at times banal universality of his attempts to escape the reality of natural law by inventing adolescent fantasies, makes the story, moreover, a dramatization not only of an aesthetic dilemma (or of the satyric satirist's paradoxical position), but of the fix Ambrose, the author-narrator, the invisible author, indeed all of us may be in.

By the time we have made our way through "Lost in the Funhouse," then, "teller, tale," and "told" have come together to emblemize the paradoxes contributing to and implicit in the artist-hero's decision to construct funhouses. Since the book is a "series," "Autobiography," and "Petition," the two pieces that fit between the three Ambrose stories, also contribute to this evolutionary process. Both "vessel and contents," teller and the tale he bears, the speaker of "Night-Sea Journey" seemingly evolves into more than one "unimaginable embodiment" of himself (12), generates not only Ambrose, and consequently the pseudo-autobiographical "Ambrose His Mark," but also "Autobiography: *A Self-Recorded Fiction.*" The first-person narrator of this "garbled or radical" "translation," this "reflection" of the tale-bearer's "reflections" ("Night-Sea Journey," 12), is the story itself, speaking of itself and existing only "in a manner of speaking" (33). A disembodied voice, "contentless form," it is a "monstrosity" sired upon a recording machine, "a mere novel device," by an author who "found himself by himself with pointless pen" (33, 35, 34). As the "bloody mirror" of its father, "upon reflection" it reverses and distorts him; as "a figure of speech" (34) it is part thing, part grammar book, and completely neither. "Being an ideal's warpèd image," its "fancy's own twist figure," it consists of words that cannot be made flesh. Still "in utero, hung up in" its "delivery," it parodies the ironic prayer of Joyce's artist-hero, Stephen Dedalus, begging its Maker to turn it off: *"Wretched old fabricator, where's your shame? Put an end to this, for pity's sake!"* (36).[22] Its plea to have its plight terminated is echoed by the monstrous correspondent of "Petition," a suicidal supplicant who signs himself "Yours truly" (68), claims to be a Siamese twin, and writes the King of Siam to ask him to become concerned with their "case" (67). Whereas Ambrose expects the sea to send him the word, the petitioner transmits a message to the "Supreme Arbiter of the Ebb and Flow of the Tide," begging him to help terminate his "freakish" (55) existence as a creature of "introspection," "revery," and "fancy" (60) attached to a lustful, beastly brother. In contrast to the speaker of "Autobiography," the petition writer wishes he had never been made flesh and ponders the paradoxes of incarnation, yet he too finds it "unspeakable" "to be both and neither" (68).

Pretending to be pure voice and found document respectively, "Autobiography" and "Petition" are signs pointing to the twin traditions Barth attempts to pull into the "Funhouse" in order that he may "have it both ways." In each case, moreover, it would appear (or sound), initially, as if the author-Maker has escaped the bind he has been put in, for he seems to have disappeared like the author of "The Revised New Syllabus" or to have traded the role of creator or narcissist for that of oracle or historian. In performance, or imagined performance, however, the father of "Autobiography" is visibly present if silent (ix) while the story refers to its mode of presentation as "a mere passing fancy who didn't pass quickly enough," a "mere" gimmick, "just in style, soon to be commonplace" (34). And if the author fails to disappear when creating an illusion of absence, so too does he foil himself when trying to hide behind a seemingly independent presence, for the fictive petitioner is revealed to be a blank, his condition may be but a monstrous metaphor, and his definition of what is the case is a blatant parody of that literary commonplace, the doppelgänger motif, that calls into question the integrity of the document by signaling the existence of a maze of intertextual relationships not only with the fiction of Makers such as Poe, Stevenson, and Nabokov, but with Barth's own. "No matter how you stand" in the mirror-room of the funhouse, "your head gets in the way."

In terms of ostensible point of view, "Autobiography" and "Petition" are the products of a process of narrative differentiation that recapitulates the evolution of narrative stances in Barth's earlier books while taking us in this one from first-person accounts, through the multiple points of view of "Lost in the Funhouse," to the indeterminate perspective of "Echo."

If "Frame-Tale" is indeed a frame-tale, then "Echo" is located in the middle of *Lost in the Funhouse*, and whereas, as critics have noted, at the center of Joyce's "Portrait of the Artist" we discover silence, at the center of Barth's, at the heart of the night-sea journeyer's Dedalian labyrinth, we encounter a completely reflective surface that confounds us with reverberations and mirror images. "Afflicted with immortality," the title character has turned "from life" and learned "to tell stories with such art that the Olympians implore her to repeat them," a decision she pays for when Hera discovers she has been deceived and punishes Echo by rendering her incapable of speaking for herself (97). As a result, in "her ultimate condition," an author's note tells us, the nymph "repeats the words of others in their own voices," and "the words of 'Echo' on the tape or the page may be regarded validly as hers," those of the other characters (Narcissus and Tiresias), the author's, "or any combination or series of the four." "Inasmuch as the three mythical principals are all more or less immortal," moreover, and Tiresias "can see both backward and forward in time, the events recounted may be already past, foreseen for the future, or in process of occurring as narrated" (x). The presence of Narcissus, the indication that Echo's transformation is a kind of punishment, and the reminder that "saturation," "telling the story over as though it were another's until . . . it loses sense," is one "cure for self-absorption" (95), all suggest that the author has not completely escaped the paradoxes of self-consciousness. Nonetheless, "Echo" is a technical tour de force in which the unseen author comes as close as he does anywhere in the book to achieving the illusion of godlike detachment espoused by Joyce's Dedalus, and which demonstrates, following Ambrose's decision to construct funhouses for others, that Barth himself possesses the ability to create for us a fictive universe where the laws of time and space need not apply.

On the other side of this looking glass, in the second half of the series, we discover a continued proliferation of perspectives and an ostensibly greater preoccupation with "the secret adventures of order." "Echo," with its numerous possible permutations of point of view, is immediately succeeded, for instance, by a pair of meditations, the "triply schizoid monologue entitled 'Title' " (x), and the six visions of "Glossolalia." Similarly, the complexity of the central tale's multiple simultaneous narratives is reflected in the Chinese boxes of "Life-Story" and the tales within tales that constitute "Menelaiad." While we may be led by this to infer that, having traced the twist in the strip, we arrive at a surface that reflects everywhere the concept that the book is an end in itself, this is not precisely the case, for in the pieces in this section of the work we still feel the tug of the tide and find signs that may be read as directing us to the visionary or the Real. To ignore rather than try to work through paradox is to accept the blindness of innocence. The Moebius strip is itself both "both and neither"; the third segment of the hero's cyclical journey concerns itself with the possibility of a return to the world.

"There's no future for prophets" (100) someone punningly says in "Echo," and the three pieces that follow it all involve soothsayings of sorts. "Two Meditations," for example, presents from a mock-omniscient point of view the propositions that the patterns that govern the universe are unpredictable and that knowledge, as Oedipus learned, always comes too late. ("To know is to recognize," Borges reminds us, "but it is necessary to have known in order to recognize, but to know is to recognize.")[23] The six "speakers in tongues" of "Glossolalia" share in common the facts "that their audiences don't understand what they're talking about" and "that their several speeches are metrically identical" (xi). Their seemingly senseless "babble, could we ken

it, might disclose a dark message, or prayer" (112), or merely a pattern of hieroglyphs cut in time. And the fictional "author" of "Title"
predicts that the "worst is to come" (102).

His schizoid *"monologue interieur"* (xi) is one of the most relentlessly
self-indulgent expressions of paralyzing self-consciousness in the series, and it is obviously informed by two of the book's regnant conceits: corpus = corpus; fiction making = love making. Experiencing
sexual "difficulties with his companion," "analogous difficulties with
the story he's in the process of composing," and believing his "culture
and its literature to be" in similar "straits" (x–xi), he has become a
naysayer fixed "in the middle, past the middle, nearer three-quarters
done, waiting for the end" (102) of his affair, his life, his story, his
culture, and the book itself. Thinking he must "Efface what can't be
faced or else fill the blank" (102), he enumerates several possibilities,
echoing some of Barth's own statements in "The Literature of Exhaustion": the "rejuvenation" of exhausted forms from their "own ashes";
the supplanting of the "moribund" by the "vigorous new"; the strategy of turning "ultimacy against itself to make something new and
valid, the essence whereof would be the impossibility of making
something new" (105–106). These alternatives, reflections of "historicity and self-awareness" (106), are voiced in counterpoint to the utterances of another voice which we may, if we like, associate with
"Her," and which points out that the fact "that some writers lack
lead in their pencils does not make writing obsolete" (108) and that
"people still fall in love, and out . . . and what goes on between
them is still not only the most interesting but the most important
thing in the bloody murderous world" (109). To go all the way with
"Her," however, is to end up "Blank," and, since the other options
are "tiresome," "unlikely," and "nauseating," the "author" continues
to narrate "himself into a corner" (108), embracing a last possibility—"Self-extinction. Silence" (106)—to indefinitely suspend his final
sentence: "How in the world will it ever   " (110). A parody of
the strategy Barth predicted Samuel Beckett would employ, this ultimate attempt to make nothing meaningful ironically makes the
"author" 's self-defeating prophecy self-fulfilling if the reader/auditor
decides mercifully to complete the sentence and fill in the blank with
the "end."

In spite of the fact that it has been occasionally quoted out of context as if it did, "Title," rather obviously, does not contain Barth's
last words on the topic, nor, for that matter, "Hers." Indeed, in the

remaining stories in the volume Barth increases the volume of "Her" selfless song, permitting "Her" in "Life-Story," for example, to interrupt the naysaying, obstruct the narrator's view of his "private legacy of awful recollection and negative resolve" ("Night-Sea Journey," 11). The hyphenated title of this piece is at least triply emblematic, suggesting not only a disjunction or a forged connection, but the linking of hierarchical levels that creates a twisted chain, in this case a potentially infinitely complex variation on what Hofstadter calls the "authorship triangle," a "Strange Loop" in which author Z exists only in a novel by author T, who exists only in a novel by E, who exists only in a novel by Z.[24] Barth's version is more baroque since the "author," a writer of novels, stories, and this life-story, both suspects that his own life is a fiction and conceives of a story containing a character who not only has the same suspicion but is writing a similar account, the situation replicating itself "in both ontological directions" potentially ad infinitum (113–14). One option he might pursue is to continue stringing out himself and his story, exhausting the possibilities one by one, but to take this route would be to sentence himself to the tedium of an endless tale "whose drama always lies in the next frame out" (117). At any point he might take a different tack and tie the tail ends of his life-story together, but because he may be "in a sense his own author, telling his story to himself" (124), this would put him in a triple bind, to say nothing of the "outside" author and reader. Taking neither to the end of the road, he instead employs a syllogism (a form of logic that may be refuted by use of a *regressus ad infinitum*)[25] to demonstrate that "the story of his life" is "a work of fact." Permitting "his real wife and imaginary mistresses" to enter "his study," he cedes control, allowing "Her" to wish him a "Happy birthday" and kiss him "to obstruct his view of the end of the sentence he" is "nearing the end of" (125–26). Illustrating that one "way to get out of a mirror-maze is to close your eyes and hold out your hands" ("Title," 108), he presumably accepts the ambiguous embrace "She" offers and "caps his pen," thereby to "end his ending story endless by interruption" (126).

When he speculates that " 'his' story" may have begun "at his birth or even generations earlier," that it may be "a *Bildungs-roman*, an *Erziehungsroman, a roman fleuve*" (122), the "author" of "Life-Story" is of course correct, for his tale is indeed part of a larger saga of formation and education, of a "stream novel" in which the tide of prose first takes us up to, and then carries us away along the course that proceeds from, Ambrose's conscious choice of vocation. Discovering that his mark is ambiguous, the message he has received a blank, resisting the sirens' instinctual refrain while doubting, perhaps, that the mermaids will sing to him, Ambrose finds himself lost in the protean labyrinth of the world and resolves regretfully but also pridefully to design funhouses "vaster by far than any yet constructed," "incredibly complex yet utterly controlled" ("Lost in the Funhouse," 93). The danger is that in attempting to escape in fear and confusion from the song of Love that may only be the summons of Death ("Night-Sea Journey," 10), he will lead himself from the heart of one mirror-maze to the center of another.

As the "self-styled narrator" (106) of "Title" and the "author" of "Life-Story" discover, it is just as possible to lament losing yourself in self-reflection or in infinite mirror rooms of your own creation, just as distressing to see yourself going on forever, as to despair at being possessed by "Her bewitchment" ("Night-Sea Journey," 11), at realizing you are at sea in creation, or that "what is 'immortal' " is "only the cyclic process of incarnation, which itself might have a beginning and an end" ("Night-Sea Journey," 8). The petitioner's fear of "coupling" and absorption (62), Ambrose's self-consciousness about sexual potency, his confusion at losing control and being unable to interpret conclusively the shifting design of the cheap tablet that is the book of the world, become on the other side of the mirror the self-absorbed artist's fear of schizophrenia, his self-consciousness about creative impotence, his distaste for the unimpassioned tedium and frustration of becoming obsessed "with pattern and design for their own sakes," ("Life-Story," 115), of possessing total control over a book that is an end in itself yet only a "warped" image of the Book itself. The tale-bearer's speculations about phylogeny and his resistance against the drive that compels him to repeat the refrain echo as the tale-teller's reflections on "historicity" and his reaction to the exhaustion that he believes condemns him to do likewise. The quest for the meaning of Making translates into the struggle to make meaning, the "horned" dilemma of being made to end into the difficulty of making an end. As the Grand Tutor in all his wisdom tells us, "our books stay reconciled, but who in modern terms can tell heads from tales?"

Caught in mid-passage through the dark tunnels of life-story, one may "abjure"—court suicide, "make no more," cap one's pen—or find a comfortable corner in which to "rehearse" "a series of last words, like an aging actress making one farewell appearance after another" ("Title," 108), stringing out an ultimate performance that terminates in a dumb show. Or else one may teach oneself to swim, to strike out or inscribe as if one could follow a line to that destination that is "the death of us, yet our salvation and resurrection; simultaneously our journey's end, mid-point, and commencement." The message of Fat May's laughter, "could we ken it," may be that the best laid strategies of silence, exile, and cunning do not alter the accuracy of the "actuarial tables" ("Life-Story," 118), that, however, much ado we may make about nothing, when all is said and done the only viable course is accepting the value, and seeking to overcome the difficulties, of achieving consummation with another, forging a bond, if only through a kenning, with lover, audience, world.

While all the tales in the series address this course and its perils in manners straightforward or circuitous, self- or subconscious, the two at the tail-end, "Menelaiad" and "Anonymiad," offer, if not a solution, at least a resolution, one that carries over from this saga-cycle to the next, from *Lost in the Funhouse* to *Chimera.* The self-mocking hero of "Menelaiad" reveals himself in many guises, both those others have made for him—"The fair-haired boy? Of the loud war cry! Leader of the people. Zeus's fosterling"—and that which he has made himself: "this isn't the voice of Menelaus; this voice *is* Menelaus, all there is of him" (127). In a vital, though sometimes overlooked, passage of "The Literature of Exhaustion," Barth, drawing on Borges, notes that a "labyrinth, after all, is a place in which, ideally, all the possibilities of choice (of direction, in this case) are embodied, and—barring special dispensation like Theseus'—must be exhausted before one reaches the heart. Where, mind, the Minotaur waits with two final possibilities: defeat and death, or victory and freedom." Unlike the favored Theseus, "Menelaus on the beach at Pharos" is "genuinely Baroque in the Borgesian spirit," for he "is *lost,* in the larger labyrinth of the world, and has got to hold fast while the Old Man of the Sea exhausts reality's frightening guises so that he may extort direction from him when Proteus returns to his 'true' self. It's a heroic enterprise, with salvation as its object—one recalls that the aim of the Histriones is to get history done with so that Jesus may come again the sooner, and that Shakespeare's heroic metamorphoses culminate not merely in a theophany but in an apotheosis."[26] In the case of Barth's version of the Homeric episode, Menelaus's struggle takes the twisted form of seven tales nesting within tales, seven frames or Chinese boxes, the outermost of which consists of Proteus, become the voice of Menelaus, telling the story of how that came to be, the story of Menelaus's tale; the rest, the tale of Menelaus's life as told by him to various auditors.

In order to explain himself and complete his life-story, Menelaus is compelled to suspend frame-tale after frame-tale and to move to the next frame in where the drama may lie, make his way toward the center of the labyrinth where the Minotaur's twin possibilities await. Although he suggests that his purpose is "Truth to tell" (130), to peel off the "cloaks of story," remove "Her" "veils" to reach "naked Helen" (140), the overwhelming question that wraps him in this argument of insidious intent is "Why me?" (150), why did Helen choose him, less than others, above all others. Telling his way away from and toward "the seed and omphalos of all" (148), he rephrases the question, asking "Who am I?" and:

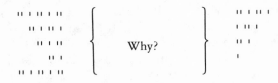

each time drawing a blank (153, 148).

The maze of story and typography through which he and we proceed is in a sense an elaborate (self)-deception or ruse, for all the voices that are so meticulously distinguished may be seen as Menelaus's or Proteus's or Barth's, or no one's, ink on pulp. At its heart lies a simple, if deceptive and ambiguous, answer:

$$\text{'' ' '' ' '' ' ''} \quad \text{Love!} \quad \text{'' ' '' ' '' ' ''}$$
$$(150)$$

But, while this is the word that can trigger the implosion of the entire edifice, Menelaus cannot take it to heart. Proteus tells him "Helen chose" him "without reason because she loves" him "without cause," advising him to "embrace her without question and watch" his "weather change" (156); Helen enjoins him to "woo" the "senseless answer to our riddle" and "espouse" her "without more carp" (159). Menelaus, however, in fear of being fooled, rejects their comebacks, holds on to himself, fills the blank by himself, and thereby loses himself, makes himself not a hero but "a fool," "chimaera, a hornèd gull" (139). Choosing to remain "undeceivèd Menelaus, solely, imperfectly" (161), he becomes not the "eternal husband" (127), but the eternal cuckold. Since he has "lost course" (128), his "voice yarns on," and "when the voice goes he'll turn tale, story of his life, to which he clings yet, whenever, how-, by whom-recounted" (161–62).

Unlike Homer's hero Menelaus (*Odyssey*, 4) and Vergil's bee-keeper, Aristaeus (*Georgics*, 4), who, assisted by nymphs and fortified by ambrosia and nectar, wrest direction from Proteus the ever-truthful, perform the proper acts of faith, and succeed, respectively, in bringing forth buzzing bees from rotting carcasses and reaching the Elysian Fields, Barth's Menelaus, his "carcass" "long wormed" (161), resides somewhere in "Hades" (128). Unwilling to trust, to let go of self-knowledge, he, or rather all that remains of him, is woven into the tangled hierarchies of a life-story that resembles in form the structure of *Lost in the Funhouse* itself. The "Old Man of the Sea," however, has the last word: "Then when as must at last every tale, all tellers, all told, Menelaus's story itself in ten or ten thousand years expires, yet I'll survive it, I, in Proteus's terrifying last disguise, Beauty's spouse's odd Elysium: the absurd, unending possibility of love" (162). His "dark message, or prayer" metamorphoses into the book's consummating tale and points, if we trust it, to the possibility of another kind of heroism, that of "the Thesean *hero*, who, confronted with Baroque reality, Baroque history, the Baroque state of his art, need *not* rehearse its possibilities to exhaustion," need "only be aware of their existence or possibility, acknowledge them, and with the aid of *very special* gifts . . . go straight through the maze to the accomplishment of his work."[27]

"Anonymiad," the last item, if we wish, in the series, is a marooned minstrel's "Last Lay," the history of a life-story that recapitulates the development of *Lost in the Funhouse*, Barth's corpus, and all of literature; the evolution of "the author," Barth's career, and homo poeticus. The "tale-bearer," at once a singular Homeric bard and all Makers, has been seduced by love and world, deceived into exile, has fallen into fits of self-consciousness, feared exhaustion, and, like many of his predecessors/descendants in the book, has faced a blank. Halfway through his story he finds "there, at the heart, never to be filled, a mere lacuna" (177). But having acknowledged the possible existence of this lake, this pit, the bottomless well of self-reflection, the gap between word and world, shifting appearance and ideal form, he

avoids drowning in Narcissus's pool, losing his way in Echo's or Proteus's caves. Leaving "unsaid" what "must be blank" (193), he goes
on through this gesture of cynicism to recount how, inspired by his
own water, he "developed a kind of coded markings to record the ut-
terance of mind and heart," and, inspired by the gods, came to
launch "his productions worldward" (186). Although distressed as he
became older by the possibilities that there might be nothing new to
say, no "new way to say the old," that "the 'immortality' of even the
noblest works" he knew might be but "a paltry thing" (188), he was
saved from the despair of Barth's "Title" character, the fate of his
Menelaus, by a water-message and a change in point of view.

Discovering a largely blank and wholly indecipherable parchment
washed up in an amphora, he was roused to "imagine that the world
contained another like" himself, "might be," indeed, "astrew with
islèd souls, become minstrels perforce, and the sea a-clink with literature" (189). Though the amphora and its ciphers may have been his
own, this mattered not, for "the principle" he decided, "was the
same: that" he "could be thus messaged, even by that stranger" his
"former self, whether or not the fact tied" him "to the world, inspired" him "to address it once again" (190). Yearning "to be relieved
of" himself, he shifted to his "only valid point of view, first person
anonymous" (192), to become, perhaps, like Borges's Shakespeare
"nothing" and "everything that all others are," no one and godlike.[28]

Buoyed up by these gestures of faith, having "taught" himself "to
swim," he was enabled, despite the void in the center, to put "Headpiece" and "Tailpiece" of his *Anonymiad* together in their container
and set "afloat" a work that may be both and neither an end in itself
and a means to an end. Praising Apollo and committing himself to
"Her" call, he calls his tale "a continuing, strange love letter" and
says he has "ceased to care whether" it "is found and read or lost in
the belly of a whale" (193). "Will anyone have learnt its name?" he
asks. "Will everyone?" "No matter," he tells us, for:

Upon this noontime of his wasting day, between the night past and the long
night to come, a noon beautiful enough to break the heart, on a lorn fair
shore a nameless minstrel
     Wrote it. (194)

The minstrel's epitaph, his testament, is both a death sentence and a
prayer that holds open the possibilities of theophany and apotheosis,

in Todd's terms, both "a gesture of temporality" and "a gesture of eternity" (*Floating Opera*, 50).

Contained within "Frame-Tale" and linked in numerous ways to the first story in the series, his last lay may be interpreted as beginning the cycle again, leading us back to retrace our way through a labyrinth we may never leave. His final words, set adrift by themselves, suggest, however, a different course. Kenned in another way, they translate into a signaling device in the hand of the "outside author" pointing to the inviolate level outside the closed and twisted loop, into signs directing us to follow the thread that spirals out of the Funhouse and through *Chimera*.

Chapter Seven
: "Treasure Me"

What we encounter, if we choose to follow the minstrel's directions, is a three-part invention in which Barth plays even further variations on the themes of consummation, the hero as artist, and the art of heroism. A composite creation consisting of the novellas "Dunyazadiad," "Perseid," and "Bellerophoniad," Barth's *Chimera* is, like its classical namesake, part lion, part goat, and part serpent; part heroism, part satire, part deception and convolution. It is a "treble beast" (223) that threatens the would-be hero not only with death but also with petrification and exhaustion. At times a "fire-breathing dragon" (223) with the power to inflame, it seems at others a "beastly fiction" that does nothing but drag on and blow hot air. He who masters it is promised to share in immortality or to be spun out "in spirate heaven" (111), but there is always the danger that, if Hermes the trickster has his way, "Chimera" can be transformed through a play on words into "kamara" (215–16), into a hermetic chamber or box within boxes. Like *Lost in the Funhouse*, *Chimera* is also "a kind of monstrous mixed metaphor" (320), for each of its constituent parts contains figures presented in the others, and like the work that preceded it, it also is governed by the "Principle of Metaphoric Means": "the investiture by the writer of as many of the elements and aspects of his fiction as possible with emblematic as well as dramatic value" (212).

Perhaps the most obvious and subtle example of this latter aspect of the sixth book Barth completed is his use of the Fibonacci sequence and the spirals it generates. As he has pointed out, for instance, in the published version of the work, each novella is approximately "1.6 times the size of the preceding novella, because that's the Fibonacci series, the golden ratio," and the "sum of the first two novellas is equivalent to the size of the third,"[1] so that the overall form of *Chimera* is roughly suggestive of both a spiral and the first three numbers in the series (1, 1, 2, 3, 5, 8 . . .). In addition, not only is the logarithmic spiral exhibited in the pattern of exposition of "Perseid," but the manner in which it is generated is emblematic of Barth's narrative strategies throughout *Chimera* (or vice versa): the Fibonacci sequence is "defined recursively" by a "pair of formulas" and grows "from two elements by a recursive rule into" an "infinite" set,[2] coming into being through a process analogous to the attempt in each of the novellas to employ doubling and recursion to generate an infinite story. Moreover, as Barth himself indicated, the pattern is not quite "completely arbitrary." Although to use it in a fiction might be construed as indulging oneself in "the secret adventures of order," the pattern in this case is a reflection, or at worst a distortion, of a design that runs throughout the natural order: "if you unwind certain marine mollusks like the chambered nautilus, for example, which unwinds in a logarithmic spiral, and keep unwinding the spiral in that same ratio, it takes on the shape of some of the great spiral galaxies, like the galaxy M-33 in Andromeda, which is part of the Perseus series of constellations."[3] Filling all three stories with mollusks, constellations, and like-shaped artifacts, Barth thus turns the spiral into both an emblem of the book's nature as the offspring of mixed parents, the product of the mating of Fact and Fancy, the Real and Ideal, and an emblem of one of the work's major themes, the chimerical nature of human freedom as manifested in the quests of his heroes and dramatized through a tension between conscious adherence to a pattern and unconscious retracing of a predetermined plot. In so doing, of course, he also, not incidentally, calls into question the "hypothetical form" and "creative detachment" of his art, employs the "Principle of Metaphoric Means" to cause us to ponder the significance of his use of concepts of order such as the "Principle of Metaphoric Means."

The original chimera, finally, was a mythic creature slain in one myth with the aid of a mythical beast born in another, by a hero whose career resembles that of the hero of that other tale: Bellerophon, whose life-story parallels in outline that of Perseus, conquered the chimera with the assistance of Pegasus, the winged steed created out of a drop of blood that fell from the head of the Gorgon killed by the son of Zeus and Danaë. It was the discovery of these connections, an intrusive authorial voice tells us in "Bellerophoniad," that was the genesis of that *"comic novella,"* a *"companion-piece to* Perseid*"* (210). More than that, however, the history of the two myths provided Barth with both a precedent for, and a vehicle for dramatizing, his own treatment of mythological matter and "the old tales."

As in "Menelaiad" and "Anonymiad," in *Chimera* Barth addresses the archetypes directly, following the procedures and achieving the effects he once enumerated to an interviewer:

Of course, when you consciously use an old myth, a received myth, like the myth of Perseus or the myth of Helen, Paris, and Menelaus, then whatever there is of the originally mythopoeic in your own imagination is either going to come in somewhere else in that text—with new characters, or language, or new twists to the old myth—or else will simply flow in to fill in those mythic receptacles which go by the names of Paris, Menelaus, Helen. I believe firmly, in other words, that some of the serious affect that we experience in the face of genuine myth can be experienced in the face of contemporary "comic" fiction using mythic materials.[4]

A number of critics have suggested that through employing such strategies Barth seeks to combat literary exhaustion by creating works that "inscribe" themselves "in the spaces opened by" earlier works, filling in some of the blanks with further play to renew the original.[5] While this may indeed be valid, the viability of what is thus created is another proposition, one of the things his novella series is "about" and the very thing his heroes go about trying to test.

"Dunyazadiad"

The first part of Barth's three-stage reclamation project, "Dunyazadiad," is a renewed telling of the "story of the story of" the "stories" (63) of his favorite taleteller, Scheherazade. Inspired by the tales within tales that make up the original, and emulating the "ifrit who steals a girl away on her wedding night" and "puts her in a treasure-casket locked with seven steel padlocks" to insure "that nobody except himself can have her" (12), Barth conjures up what may be read as basically "*seven* concentric stories-within-stories, so arranged" that, given the right degree of "passionate virtuosity," the "climax of the innermost would precipitate that of the next tale out, and that of the next, et cetera . . ." (32).[6] One way he adds "new twists" to the received text is to evoke a number of "Strange Loops" on the order of Borges's version of Scheherazade's six hundred and second night. Most of these are brought about by the entrance into the novella of a genie whose appearance and biography are very similar to Barth's and who, among other things, having read *The Thousand and One Nights,* conveys to Scheherazade the stories she will recite to Shahryar, making her "original" telling a retelling. Like the locks on the selfish ifrit's casket, such loops can, if we permit them, keep the treasure casket closed, the novella self-contained and self-referential. If we break them, however, or open them with the proper key, then we may experience a climax and discover that "Dunyazadiad" directs us to the mortal and Real, the inviolate level where the "outside author" resides, and to the immortal and Ideal, the heaven of ideas wherein resides the book called *The Thousand and One Nights*.

When we directly pick up the thread that leads from "Anonymiad" to *Chimera,* we find that the "noontime" of the minstrel's "wasting day" has become the wedding night of Scheherazade and Shahryar, her sister and Shah Zaman. Grossly simplified and rendered linear, the first part of the first novella consists of a rehearsal of the background to the ground situation, and of the genesis and delivery, of the tales of *The Thousand and One Nights*. Here Barth further renews his source and taps a source of renewal by mixing in seeming anachronisms, colloquial diction, and double entendres, and especially by making the predominant point of view that of Sherry's kid sister Dunyazade or Doony.

As she tells it, seeking a way to put an end to "Shahryar's virgin-a-night policy" (14), "as a last resort" Scheherazade "turned to her first love," "mythology and folklore," discovering that the "magic" is always "in words," in understanding "which words work, and when, and for what" (15). Learning that "the trick is to learn the trick," Sherry did. For from imagining that their "situation" was "the plot of a story" she and her sister were reading, she concluded that the "magic" must come "down to the particular words in the story" and stated that "It's as if—as if the key to the treasure *is* the treasure," thereby summoning the genie who provided her with the key to turning death into almost death (15–16). Drawn into their stories in the same instant that "he set on paper the words *The key to the treasure is the treasure*" (19), the Genie delivered both the means of arresting Shahryar and a lecture in which he averred that his "experience of love gone sour only made him treasure more highly the notion of a love that time would season and improve," asserting, "If love died it died; while it lived, let it live forever" (24–25). By the time we reach the end of the first part of the novella, however, it becomes clear that the two women had rejected the Genie's faith in "the absurd, unending possibility of love." Considering him "either a liar or a fool" in such matters (45), they had hatched a plot to gain revenge through a "reversal not only of the genders of teller and told" (masculine and feminine in the Genie's terms) but also "of their circumstances" (47), and Dunyazade, we learn, has been telling her story to a bound Shah Zaman whom she believes she has at her mercy.

Part 2, narrated by a third person, contains the King's appeal. Demonstrating that he deliberately put himself in her hands, he exhibits his trust by taking away and restoring her power to unsex him. Entreating Dunyazade to permit him to tell his own story, he reveals that he learned through love and impotence something that the responsive reader may already have suspected: the true magic words are "*as if*," words "which, to a person satisfied with seeming, are more potent than all the genii in the tales" (57). Acknowledging that "it's absurd," he nevertheless suggests that they "make a philosophy of that *as if*" "make love" *as if* they were "passionate equals" for as long as they can (63, 62). Whether or not Dunyazade can accept what Barth's Menelaus could not and can answer the King's plea ("Treasure me!") is a matter of conjecture; the last line of dialogue leaves us with Shah Zaman's wish that they share in wishing each other "Good morning!" (63).

The voice that speaks the third, and potentially eternally penultimate, part of the novella belongs to neither king nor vizier's daughter but to someone playing the role of author. After describing the marriage and bequest that end *Alf Laylah Wa Laylah,* the book that exists somewhere, he says if he "could invent a story as beautiful, it should be about little Dunyazade and her bridegroom, who pass a thousand nights in one dark night and in the morning embrace each other; they make love side by side, their faces close, and go out to greet sister and brother in the forenoon of a new life." The story is one he cannot conclude, he tells us, yet "it must end in the night that all good mornings come to" when, like all things, it is taken by what the "Arab storytellers" called "the Destroyer of Delights and Desolator of Dwellingplaces" (64). If, however, we can accept the "as if" he offers, then this "denouement" may indeed become a moment of "untying" in which the tangled loops of story are opened up, a joyous climax that occurs concurrently in all the frames of the tale.

"Perseid"

No matter which we choose, the dark night or the good morning, if we read on we find ourselves in the good night during which Perseus, having achieved stardom, tells "to those with eyes to see and understanding to interpret," the story he has become and "nightly" rehearses for "as long as men and women read the stars" (142). His "patterned tale" (67), "Perseid," is a continuous tape perpetually rewound, unwound, and replayed. It is a dialogue containing a monologue containing a dialogue, in which the "estellated" hero awakes each night "to think" himself "beworlded and find" himself "in heaven" and then reviews for his heavenly companion, Medusa, "the night" he "woke to think and find" himself "vice-versa" (67).

Having become "long lost, deserted," "sea-leveled, forty," and "beleaguered by the serpents of" his "past" (67), he awakened "in the middle of the story of" his "life (68) to find himself in the company of the nymph Calyxa. Because he previously had tried to erase all, "clean the slate altogether" (68), to remember who he was it was necessary for him to recount the earlier chapters of his life-story, aided by a series of murals graven on the walls of his marble recovery room. Forming what appeared to be an infinitely unwinding spiral, "like the triton-shell that Dedalus threaded for Cocalus" (69), the temple displayed on its walls panels depicting episodes from Perseus's myth, arranged in such a way that the key incidents from the first half of his life carved along the first whorl were aligned with corresponding adventures from the second half depicted along the second. These murals, of course, are among the principal things that make "Perseid" "patterned"—both elaborately "designed" and "imitative"—for the elegant structure they comprise is seemingly self-replicating, and the reliefs themselves, Barth has indicated, were inspired by Dido's frescoes in the second book of the *Aeneid*.[7]

Reviewing the early chapters of his story while discovering his impotence with Calyxa, Perseus recalled that the heroic deeds recorded in official versions of his myth had left him feeling "fettered and coffered as ever by Danaë's womb, the brass-bound chest, Polydectes's tasks," fearing with "half a life to go" that he was "petrifying" (79). In order to rediscover his direction, he had adopted, therefore, a program of retracing his "good young days" to "find the key" (80), had attempted to discover "whether" he "felt" his "post-Medusan years an example of or an exception to the archetypal pattern for heroic adventure" (88). Thinking "to overtake with understanding" his "present paragraph as it were by examining" his "paged past, and, thus pointed, proceed serene to the future's sentence" (88–89), he had learned instead that "the case was truly altered" (99).

Remembering that, like the Goat-Boy, he had failed in his effort to turn this knowledge into a successful program based upon the negation of previous actions, he left Calyxa, resolved that his "second tale" should "be truly a second, not mere replication of" his "first" (121). His potency at least partially restored by the nymph, he went on to slay not only his remaining enemies but also "unpleasant middle Perseus" (132) and to confront a New Medusa, who supposedly had been given back her erstwhile beauty and granted the new power to turn both herself and her true lover "ageless as the stars" (115). Proving that he had shifted his faith from Athene to Aphrodite, and that he, unlike Menelaus, could find it possible to trust, he cast aside his fear of petrification, "slipped back" Medusa's "problematic cowl," and staring into her eyes was transfigured into his present, semi-eternal state (134).

In the last paragraphs of his "new story" ("novella" in Italian), Perseus claims that he is "content." Although his "fate is to be able only to imagine boundless beauty from" his "experience of boundless love," he says he is satisfied with that "as if," for he has "a fair imagination to work with, and, to work from, one priceless piece of unimagined evidence," that he holds "above *Beta Persei*" not "serpents but lovely woman's hair" (142). Nevertheless, some of the words the starry-eyed lovers exchange during the question and answer period that concludes their nightly course can be interpreted as qualifying both the novella's climax and its hero's acceptance of his final condition. In Medusa, Perseus may have lovingly uncovered his "sweet salvatrix" (136), but she is critical and jealous and distrusts his choice, wonders if his kiss might have been "in complete bad faith: an act not of love but of suicide, or a desperate impulse to immortality-by-petrification" (140). Moreover, the playful, ribald language he uses in describing his stay with Calyxa is transformed in these latter passages into a style that verges, as Medusa herself notes, on the overly "mannered" (136), something that can be read as a comment about what he has given up in choosing "spirate heaven" over the nymph's "spiriferate" navel (75–76). Indeed, while the innocent Medusa states she is "glad to be out" of "the whole wretched world down there" (136), Perseus seems less certain, is curious about the fate of their "mortal parts" (141), regrets that he can never see his lover, can "feel nothing" of her but her "hair" (139). He may have won immortality and a vision of "miraculous, yes blinding love" (141), but he also feels that he has lost something of value. "Perseid," after all, is not only the name of this hero's tale but the name of a meteor shower, and his account of his elevation is, in some sense at least, ironically also the story of a fall.

"Bellerophoniad"

If "Perseid" is the first of the two works Dunyazade's genie says he is writing, novellas about "mythic heroes, true and false" (36), "Bellerophoniad" is the second. Whereas the creator of the former affects the roles of satyr and romancer, employing a style that is at times playful, at others trite, the author of the latter plays the parts of satirist and parodist, affecting a style that is often tedious and pedantic, and betrays the fact that he lacks lead in his pencil. And while the "true" Perseus is a hero of the Thesean type who resolves to avoid rehearsing the pattern of his reality, choosing instead the path straight through the heart in order to discover who he is and reach, through special dispensation, the ambiguous consummation of his labors, the "false" Bellerophon takes an approach that is pseudobaroque, tries to exhaust the possibilities of a pattern he imposes, only to discover who he is not, reach the realization that his life-story is full of "lacunae" (320), the record of a mitigated failure to connect.

In overall form and narrative structure, "Bellerophoniad" imitates both "Perseid" and "Dunyazadiad," passes itself off as a three-part novella in which a monologue becomes a dialogue, a one-part myth in which the hero recounts to his ultimate mate the recapitulation of his prior history with a former lover. What we are finally led to believe, however, is that it is none of these things, but rather the shape-shifter Polyeidus become Bellerophon in "*Bellerophoniad*-form: a certain number of printed pages in a language not untouched by Greek, to be read by a limited number of 'Americans,' not all of whom will finish or enjoy them" (319). As such, "Bellerophoniad" is really neither monologue nor dialogue, not "Bellerus's voice" (277) speaking to us or anyone's "mortal speech," but "written words," "Bellerophonic letters afloat between two worlds, forever betraying, in combinations and recombinations, the man they forever represent" (145–46). The pattern that governs it is not any consciously imposed by hero or mortal maker but the senseless ebb and flow of the tidewater. Its author may be anyone "who has ever written or will write about the myth of Bellerophon and Chimera" (246), and because Polyeidus is both it and a character in it, both he and "Bellerophoniad" change into an assortment of non-"Bellerophonic" documents, including a copy of Robert Graves's summary of the myth of Bellerophon, a group of letters from one Jerome Bray addressed to King George III and Todd Andrews, and a schema depicting the pattern of the "monomyth."

The star of this mock myth is necessarily a phony who by "imitating perfectly the Pattern of Mythic Heroism" became "a perfect imitation of a mythic hero" (308). Having placed his faith in Athene, not Aphrodite, and having conned himself, with Polyeidus's assistance, into believing that the key to proving himself a demigod lay in satisfying the "Pattern," he spent the first part of his life forcing that design on experience, achieving potency only through rape. Proceeding, as per Polyeidus's instruction, "in keeping with the classic pattern of ascending unlikelihood" (230–31), he dispatched Chimera with a "special spear," a "version of" a "writing-tool" which "instead of a sharp bronze point had a dull one of lead" (235). The fruits of his labors, however, were only "a blurred silhouette in soot of what" he "took to be the beast itself" (237), and his winning "the devotion of" his "wife, the respect of" his "children, the esteem of" his "subjects, the admiration of" his "friends, and the fear of" his "enemies," all of which argued "the protection of Olympus" at a time "when your typical authentic mythic hero finds himself suddenly fallen from the favor of gods and men," thereby proving his "fraudulent nature" (243).

Discovering "at sundown on the eve of his birthday" a "Greek novella called *Perseid,* story of his model hero" (145), he went through it and found himself suffering from exhaustion. The cure, he became convinced, was to "do the second-cycle thing like Perseus," "to follow the Pattern" and "get Pegasus off the ground" (269). But, although he tried by this means to tack on and to a happy ending to his story, the result was merely "suspended animation" (305) until he proposed that myth "could be so much realer and more important than particular men that perhaps" he "must cease to be the hero of" his "own, cease even to exist, cease somehow even to have existed" (305–6). Realizing this, he made sad and fierce love with his imagined auditor, Melanippe; received her boon, the magical hallucinatory herb, hippomanes; and took off to slay "the chimera of" his "life" by concluding that it was not "mortal" him, but "immortality," that "was the myth" (315), that Bellerophon's fame "is as it were anonymous" (317), and that Chimera is "*not* a great invention," "not monstrous" but "preposterous," "its death" the "only mythopoeic thing about it" (316).

Theretofore, his story had been one of "confusion and fiasco," an imitation that amused the gods. At that point, however, Zeus ceased to be amused, for Bellerophon was "high enough" to see "Mystery and Tragedy plain": "Mystery in the hero's journey to the other world, his illumination, his transcension of categories, his special dispensation; Tragedy in his return to daily reality, the necessary loss in his translation of the ineffable into sentences and cities, his fall from the favor of gods and men, his exile, and the rest" (308–9). Polyeidus as gadfly-cum-deus ex machina was therefore employed to put both horse and rider "over the old finish-line" (311) by sending both plummeting. Cushioning his own fall by "plotting," he changed into the story's "fluttering final pages" (312), into "the last words" he permits Bellerophon to deliver "to the world at large": "It's no *Bellerophoniad*. It's a   " (319–20).

Chimera

To those familiar with the Goat-Boy's efforts to exercise free will to alter the laws of his university, his attempt to enter a program designed to produce a Grand Tutor, much of *Chimera* may seem like reiteration. Systems are once again satirized, free choice once again leads to ironic or paradoxical ends. Perseus decides to break out of the pattern of his story and embrace "the compound predications of commitment" (134), only to end up proving that he is "ineluctably" a "bloody mythic hero" (132). Bellerophon remains to the end committed to the Pattern for which Perseus's story is one model, wishes to become transformed into "an immortal *Bellerophoniad,*" into a perfect and permanent form, but he will survive only for a limited time in the "ill-proportioned" recombinant novella Polyeidus has turned into (318, 319). In both cases *"the mortal desire for immortality"* finds *"its ironically qualified fulfillment"* (207), and in both tales "the Destroyer of Delights and Desolator of Dwellingplaces" claims the opening and closing words. The heroes' "fame" is at best "anonymous"—"it's hardly to be imagined that those patterns we call 'Perseus,' 'Medusa,' 'Pegasus' . . . are aware of their existences, any more than are their lettered counterparts on the page. Or, if by some mystery they are" (as in "Perseid"), "that they enjoy their fixed, frigidified careers" (317). Perseus's career is at once transcendent and meteoric; before he is sent spiraling downward, Bellerophon accomplishes his labors by transcending them. As they affect the ultimate disposition of the heroes' "mortal parts," the distinctions between "true" and "false," passage and failure, are certainly irrelevant.

It would appear, then, that Barth has reconstructed a spiral edifice in "Perseid" only to dismantle it in and through "Bellerophoniad" and expose the abyss, the blank, beneath. To read the latter after the former is to reread the former in terms of the latter, to conclude, perhaps, that the immortality of "Perseid" is also a myth, for although "some stories last longer than others" (145), and "stories last longer than men," "stones" last longer than "stories, stars than stones" (67). If "Bellerophoniad" is a protean and Polyeidic imitation, so to an extent is "Perseid," and both may be full of lacunae, may be nothing more or less than monstrous mixed metaphors, collections of "silent, visible signs" (142) or "Bellerophonic letters afloat between two worlds, forever betraying" the men they represent as they are subjected to interpretation, reinterpretation, or misinterpretation, as they are combined and recombined in innumerable acts of reading.

However, whereas *Lost in the Funhouse* draws on the *Künstlerroman* and the myth of the artist-as-hero to depict the types of heroism and the possibilities of consummation, *Chimera* employs myth and sexual relationships to portray the role of the artist, and in terms of that performance, Barth's novella sequence, like his story series, climaxes not with dissolution but with a resolution. Both books in their own ways continue and expand the dramatization of the author's tragisatiric position begun in *Giles,* carrying it both back and forward in an effort to expose the implications of the aesthetic and epistemology that underlie the earlier fiction while moving from tragic limitation and satiric isolation to comic reconciliation. Brought to the fore and taken to the end of the road, the undermining of the foundations of realism enacted in Barth's first two works, for instance, culminates in Ambrose's disappointment in his "water-message," in the disorientation experienced by the narrator and protagonist of "Lost in the Funhouse." Similarly, the undermining of authority initiated in *Giles* leads, when approached self-consciously, to the frustration of the mortal desire for immortality, to anonymity, the impotence of the glossolalists and Tiresias in his cave; the attempt to reorchestrate past conventions in rewriting Cooke's history to the paralyzing sense of historicity and fear of literary exhaustion that afflict the author of "Title." Having pushed language beyond sense to create play and played with plotting elaborate patterns in both *Sot-Weed* and "The Revised New Syllabus," Barth presents us with the artist-hero's ambiguous reaction to the discovery that his mark is ambiguous, the hieroglyphs are indecipherable, with elaborately designed "Strange Loops" that threaten to succeed in putting the "outside" author in a literary bind while failing to free him from the temporal bind he is literally in. Having decided in one of his roles to circumnavigate the problem of choosing between Scylla and Charybdis by fleeing from the whole monstrous bloody world, the author finds himself in the "Funhouse" facing the difficulty of charting a course between a Bellerophonic urge to impose, adhere to, and exhaust a grandiose design and a Polyeidic propensity for shape-shifting.

At one point in "Dunyazadiad," the Genie, who believes he is "going in circles," has "lost track" of who he is and cannot find "the key" to the "code," states that his project "is to learn where to go by discovering where" he is "by reviewing where" he's "been—where we've *all* been" (18), and this, of course, is indeed the scenario acted out in the course of *Chimera* as the drama is replayed, following the thread that leads from the "Funhouse" to Barth's later works, rediscovering, clarifying, and revalidating the directions inscribed in "Anonymiad" through a comparison of not only the ultimate fate of his mythic heroes but also the relative viability of their respective tales. Looked at in one way, "Perseid" and "Bellerophoniad" constitute the construction by metaphoric means of a historical portrait of the artist that seems to reconfirm many of the worst fears about exhaustion and ultimacy expressed by various author figures in *Lost in the Funhouse*: Perseus becomes immortalized, his story a lasting myth, because he and it are primary inventions, because he exists in a world and time where he can recover his self-confidence and find an auditor who believes in mythic heroes; Bellerophon dies "to immortality" (145), becomes a story that is less lasting, because his invention is not original, because he is aware that all he can do is repeat a pattern, parody a model, that in his time neither he nor the populace can believe in his heroism. Looked at in another way, of course, both novellas are imitations that explore different paths the postmodern writer may take, different ways of dramatizing his situation. Taken on these terms, "Bellerophoniad" is an intentional failure which reveals that, for the artist as well as the hero, self-knowledge is bad news, that too much understanding of what one is up to can leave one mired, too great an awareness of historicity can stifle spontaneity and lead one to settle for and into leaden parody, and that the writer, like Bellerophon, can achieve only limited flight by arriving at a tragic view of his own situation and turning ultimacy against itself. "Perseid," on the other hand, seems to demonstrate that a lesser degree of self-consciousness may permit greater success, produce a more lively and long-lived tale, and that the way to recover potency is not to be petrified by or repeat the patterns of the past, but somehow to begin again confident that one's tale will be more than a mere replication.

These two mythic and metaphorical novellas do not, however, contain the full story of the story. No matter how successful it is, "Perseid" will always be followed and undercut by the "nay-saying" of "Bellerophoniad," and neither piece very explicitly explains the *means* by which the artist-hero may free himself of self-consciousness and historicity to put lead back in his pencil, may face what Bellerophon and Polyeidus know and still aspire to be a Perseus or go on to write "Perseid." To completely decipher the code, therefore, we must end Bellerophon's suspended sentence, connect his last words to "Dunyazadiad."

As the story goes, a story supported by evidence in the text itself, Barth originally intended to end *Chimera* with "Dunyazadiad,"[8] but was persuaded by his editor to alter the sequence. Were the book arranged in this manner (if only in the heaven of ideas), the successful climax of Dunyazade's tale not only would entail the climaxes of all seven frames of her novella but also would precipitate the successful consummation of all seven sections of *Chimera* as a whole, a consummation that would involve the fulfillment of both Doony's relationship with Shah Zaman and the author's relationship with the reader. According to Borges, "a book is more than a verbal structure," it "is the dialogue with the reader,"[9] and according to Barth's genie, who reiterates the analogy between lovemaking and storytelling developed in *Lost in the Funhouse,* that dialogue may be described in sexual terms: "The teller's role, he felt, regardless of his actual gender, was essentially masculine, the listener's or reader's feminine, and the tale was the medium of their intercourse" (34). The key, thus, to a satisfying denouement, whether we are talking about Dunyazade's wedding morning or her tale, is the partners' willingness to accept the notion that they can "make love like passionate equals," and the magic words in each case are Shah Zaman's *"as if."*

Both Doony and the King, the Genie notes with alarm, face the possible menace of exhaustion: she has "had the whole literary tradition" as well as "the whole erotic tradition" transmitted to her; he, quite probably, has heard all the stories there are to tell, made love in all the possible ways (40–41). Both, moreover, know that love cannot last forever, that nothing "works" (61), and although he maintains ultimate control over the situation, if he freely chooses to place "his life in" her "hands," she may "cut him off entirely" ("Life-Story," 124). Yet each of them in a way is a virgin, for Dunyazade has only experienced heterosexual love vicariously, and, while Shah Zaman has exhausted the charm of novelty, he has never been truly "possessed" by anything "but despair" (60). And even though they are both sophisticated, because they are also both in a sense innocent, their world still contains room and time for passionate virtuosity if they can agree, in full awareness of what they know to be the case, to be "satisfied with seeming," make love *as if* they "were equals" for "as long as" they "can."

The anonymous minstrel's gesture of faith, his decision to imagine that the sea "might be astrew" with other minstrels, is modified, then, in "Dunyazadiad" into the resolution to go on as if the world were filled with potential lovers, his "dark message, or prayer" into the King's plea: "Treasure me . . . as I'll treasure you!" (61). The keys to such treasuring, we discover, are a willingness to believe in "the truly tragic view of love" (61), a satyric acceptance of limitation, a satiric rejection of absolutes, and a heroic resolve to accomplish one's labors by transcending them. The "masculine" partner, whether paramour or storyteller, must trust enough in the existence of his lover to overcome his obsession with his stranded state in order that he may trust that hypothetical lover enough to permit him to forego attempting Bellerophonic rape, may trust himself enough to regain his potency by conquering his petrifying self-consciousness about what he is up to. In turn, his "feminine" mate must join him in embracing the belief that "fictions" can be "truer than fact" (61), in agreeing to hold on to their sophistication while making the most of their innocence, and in pledging mutual faith in spite of the fact that both he and she suspect that there is much which must be "left unsaid," much which "must be blank." "To be joyous in the full acceptance of this dénouement is surely to possess a treasure, the key to which is the understanding that Key and Treasure are the same" (64). For, by taking to heart the magic words, both author and auditor may rediscover the magic of words, unlocking the treasury that is the thesaurus, the storehouse that is the literary tradition, may learn that the writer's reward is not immortality but the pleasure of writing, the reader's reward not truth but the pleasure of reading, may come to feel that although nothing ultimately works, their joint "enterprise is noble," "full of joy and life," while "the other ways are deathy" (61–62).

Realizing that "the trick is to learn the trick," and learning it by finding that the magic "comes down to particular words in the story" he is in, the author of "Dunyazadiad" makes use of the "Principle of Metaphoric Means" to write himself out of the corner he had written himself into and get back on track at the same time that he tells Doony's new and delightful, if endless, tale. In the best of all possible worlds, *Chimera* would conclude with his closing words to his "little sister" (64), with a potential breaking of circles, opening up of locks, with the promise of a continuing dialogue infinitely spinning "a catherine-wheel or whirling galaxy, a golden shower of fiction" (26). That this is not the case, however, is no great matter, for the reader may fill in the blank left by "Bellerophoniad" with the thousand nights and good morning to be found at the book's beginning and view that return as more than mere recapitulation, may choose to see the work's spiral form as an emblem not of serpentine convolution but of the future unfolding of promising possibilities. Polyeidus, after all, leaves a part of himself behind when he comes to be bound in those "Bellerophonic letters" mired in a Maryland marsh, but by doing so he gains the freedom "to operate in a few aspects of" his "own" (319), to become the characters, assume the form, of an utterly new and revolutionary novel that sounds in his description a good deal like *LETTERS*.

Chapter Eight

Reading, Writing, 'Rithmetic: Revolution, Replenishment, Romance

In a way, *Lost in the Funhouse* and *Chimera,* widely considered to be Barth's most experimental and self-reflexive works, are also both topical and traditional. The experimentation with modes of presentation, the self-consciousness and self-reference, the attitudes toward language, literature, and historicity that characterize the books, after all, refer us to a specific historical ambiance, to not only the "felt ultimacies" but the fashionable linguistic and critical theories of the period in which they were written. Barth's experiments with recordings, for instance, may be seen as reflections of and on the endeavors of those "intermedia colleagues" he mentions in "The Literature of Exhaustion," as responses to the McLuhanites' challenge to the "print-oriented bastard."[1] Viewed and described in the context of contemporary critical inquiry, furthermore, his exploitation of combinations of "technologies" in *Lost in the Funhouse* becomes, in the words of Charles Caramello, an oscillation "between a search for the grounded self in 'speech' and a belief in the dispersed selves of 'writing.' "[2]

Like the events recorded on George's endless reels, however, Barth's toying with tapes is a rebellion along traditional lines, an attempt to avoid linearity that leads to an acceptance of that which is essentially and inevitably linear, and as is the case with *Giles Goat-Boy,* in *Lost in the Funhouse* and *Chimera* that which is of topical or technical interest is made to address matters more universal as it is incorporated into the allegory. For, whether or not Barth's multimedia presentations are successful efforts to escape the limitations of print and successive time, they are "monstrous" and "deathy," take us to Echo's cave, fix us in the perpetually stillborn moment of "Autobiography," while failing to release their temporally bound recorder. "Multiplying the possible channels of speech, decentering the place of voice," Barth, Caramello points out, does not necessarily "deny *some* authority at the origin of" his "multiple voices," just as in tracing his tangled hierarchies he does not deny the existence of an inviolate level beyond them. The "performing self" recording speech or writing books "remains very concrete . . . and mortal," and failing to negate this ultimate fact or "obviate Barth's need to stage his continuing appearance in the world of letters,"[3] the performances of *Lost in the Funhouse* are subsumed into a mythic pattern of return that leads Barth back to the traditional, through the recontacting of the "original springs of narrative" (17) in "Dunyazadiad" to a recommitment to print and linearity manifested in the subtitles of his later works—*LETTERS: A Novel* and *Sabbatical: A Romance*.

What is true of his experiments with new media, moreover, also applies to other of those aspects of *Lost in the Funhouse* and *Chimera* that seem to be products of a particular ambiance. For, using myth and very conventional conceits, such as the equations between corpus and corpus, the created book and the Book of creation, Barth in both works turned the fashionable practice of writing about writing into a metaphor for other forms of self-examination and inquiry, moving from the topical to the archetypal and continuing his own past practice of relating aesthetics to ethics and metaphysics. Employing, lampooning, and transcending the principles of the literature of exhausted possibility, he ended up effecting a Thesean escape, impelled by an evolved sense of audience and an altered attitude toward patterns and patterning. Responding to the apocalyptic tenor of the times and to the modernist tradition, he managed, in short, to create a pair of books that both exemplify and helped make possible the program for a postmodernist fiction he has called "a literature of replenishment," a program carried forward in *LETTERS* and *Sabbatical*.

To become better attuned to the revitalized relationship between the three terms of storytelling that evolves out of *Chimera* and realize the extent to which it is consonant with ideas sounded out in "The Literature of Replenishment," one need only turn to some of the remarks Barth has made about the roles of the reader and author of his next two texts. In a 1979 interview that focused primarily on the recently published *LETTERS* but also included discussion of his initial plans for what would become *Sabbatical*, Barth indicated that as he grew "older and perhaps wiser," he found himself "putting some respectful distances between" himself and the "modernist masters," one of which "involves" the rapport between him and his audience. "When" he is "asked whom" he writes for or "who" his "reader is," he said, he "no longer" regards "that as a dopey question—although" he "probably did when" he "was in" his "twenties and thirties." A "writer, if he's lucky," he elaborated, "will be aware of that delicate point where he had better not tax the reader's patience too much. Just as a juggler has to control the number of tenpins in the air or an acrobatic team has to monitor the number of performers on the wire, an author has to avoid introducing that final complication which will bring his reader to a point where he or she says, 'That's just one avatar too many.' "[4]

LETTERS

Going on to suggest how this applies to *LETTERS*, Barth made several statements that seem to be very much in harmony with the spirit of his essay on postmodernism, where he alludes to the possibility of steering a course between the position of Bertolt Brecht, who allegedly "kept on his writing desk a toy donkey bearing the sign *Even I must understand it*" and that of the "high modernists" who "might aptly have put on their desks a professor of literature doll bearing, unless its specialty happened to be the literature of high modernism, the sign *Not even I can understand it*."[5] Telling his interviewer that he considers his seventh book and third "big book" to be, if not "a Swiss watch," "at least a respectable Switzerland cuckoo clock where all the cogs and pendulums actually do engage," Barth implied that he is more concerned that it work for the reader than that he or she perceive all the intricacies of its works. Rather than representing the kind of work "that has to be studied like a Nabokovian production," it is, he asserted, "the kind of novel where if one is charmed by Lady Amherst and not so charmed by A. B. Cook" (two of its principals), "one could more or less skim through the Cook passages. You might not get precisely the same assemblage, but I think you would emerge with a sound sense of what is going on in the overall novel." Proposing, additionally, that "the best way to read" *LETTERS* is to move through it linearly, even though this is complicated by its departures from "chronological order," he also declared quite indulgently that he does not "think much is lost if the reader devises his own method and sticks to it."[6]

Since the book is a "second cycle" novel, preceded not only by the ontology and literary ontogeny of the cycle of works that Barth created in the first half of his life but also by the "reenactment" of his "paged past" in *Chimera,* and since all the earlier works are not only informed by but "about" particular attitudes toward patterns and patterning, or efforts to inscribe or interpret *the* Pattern, the revolutionary concept of the interdependence of teller, tale, and told that motivates *LETTERS* is informed by evolutionary approaches to composition, interpretation, and revelation. Moreover, just as Borges's comments about literary intercourse seem to be reflected in Barth's novella series, so, too, does it appear that some of his reflections on design are mirrored in the fiction Barth produced after it. In the same essay in which he speaks of literature as an infinite dialogue with the reader, Borges tells us that at "the end of the thirteenth century Raymond Lully . . . attempted to solve all the mysteries by means of a frame with unequal, revolving, concentric disks, subdivided into sectors with Latin words," that at "the beginning of the nineteenth century John Stuart Mill expressed the fear that the number of musical combinations would some day be exhausted," and that "at the end of the nineteenth century Kurd Lasswitz played with the overwhelming fantasy of a universal library that would record all the variations of the twenty-odd orthographic symbols." Such fears and conceptions he argues "may make us laugh, but they merely exaggerate a common propensity to consider metaphysics and the arts as a sort of combinatory game," a propensity that also leads one to reduce "the universe" to "a manifestation of chance," to "transform each one of us into the interesting interlocutor of a secret and continuous dialogue with nothingness or with divinity." This kind of game-playing, he pronounces, "at bottom" flatters "the vanity," and is therefore, in a sense, "immoral."[7]

Barth, of course, considers Borges to be not only a model modernist but also "a bridge between the end of the nineteenth century and the end of the twentieth,"[8] and the proclivities the Argentine thus descries on the way toward affirming the value of Bernard Shaw's ethical and liberating work are burlesqued by Barth through his depiction of Jerome Bray, a relative of the Goat-Boy's nemesis who first appears in *Chimera* and reappears in *LETTERS.* One of the documents Polyeidus turns into in "Bellerophoniad" is a letter in which this insectile character explains his computer-assisted program for the *"Second Phase of Composition of"* a *"Revolutionary Novel* NOTES" (256). Confused in his mind with "a Novel Revolution," this "scientific fiction" (259),

Bray believes, will redeem the failure of the first phase of his project, in which his efforts to create "the 'Complete,' the 'Final Fiction' " (260) and bring about the consummation of Kabbalistic tradition, resulted in a "printout" that "was no masterwork but an alphabetical chaos, a mere prodigious jumble of letters" entitled *NUMBERS* (262). Inasmuch "as 'character,' 'plot,' and for that matter 'content,' 'subject,' and 'meaning,' are attributes of particular novels," *NOTES* "is to dispense with all of" these "in order to transcend the limitations of particularity; like the coded *NUMBERS* it will represent nothing beyond itself, have no content except its own form, no subject but its own processes. Language itself it will perhaps eschew" (266).

In *LETTERS,* Jerome Bonaparte Bray's letters to "The Author" and others reveal him to be wrapped up in similar programming, but here the sequencing has apparently been reversed, for the literary technologist and his biomechanical computer, LILYVAC, progress from *NOVEL* to *NOTES* through "*Blank* Illuminations" to *NUMBERS,* "the world's 1st work of Numerature." Delivering "a parting shot" to that "exhausted medium," his projected project will make an "end to letters," win him swarms of "*numerati,*" and "revolutionize Revolution." Freed from "Literature's limitations" he and his work will be placed "as far beyond" the "Author's," or anyone's "grasp as was Bellerophon past Chimera's when he flew on mighty Pegasus to his rendezvous with the Godblank."[9] Since the epistle in "Bellerophoniad" postdates the ones in *LETTERS,* however, if we can trust the documentary evidence and can view Barth's books as forming a continuum, Bray may be trapped in a recursive and recurrent nightmare, condemned because of a tangle in his programming to review perpetually the past only to reenact a progression that leads back to future regression. His own analogy may be more apt than he supposes, for since he is akin to Barth's Bellerophon, this ultimately paranoid priest of ultimacy may be fated to forever betray himself through his own combinations and recombinations.

Like Ambrose and the author who transmits George's allegory, this J. B. is an avatar of "The Author," a Polyeidic gadfly who by engaging in combinatory games, dialogues with divinity and nothingness, lampoons the artist-hero's own fears and conceptions, his confrontations with exhaustion and Bellerophonic self-betrayal, his flirtations with formalism, numerology, and technology. This puncturing of artifice and aspirations may portend a fall back down to earth, but it is also a Quixotic bit of transcendent self-parody that takes us back to where the genre began, a necessary rehearsal and acknowledgment of limitations that makes possible the possibility of an infinite dialogue with the reader. Bray's correspondence may suggest correspondences between his computer printout and Barth's cuckoo clock, but "The Author" of *LETTERS* does not share Bray's Napoleonic middle name, and there are indeed significant differences between Bray's program and Barth's design, not the least of which is that while the former may be an infinite loop, the latter describes itself as, among other things, a double spiral, a musical score, a perpetual calendar, and a brachiating tree of life.

At one point in his plotting, Bray calculates that the task before him can be equated with finding "the key" to "a *leafy anagram* of monstrous proportions" that may "itself" be regarded as "the acrostic for a much larger text" (331), and this description of efforts to figure out the universe, we discover in the course of reading, is in some ways an apt trope for the task we ourselves become engaged in if we join him in attempting to decode the fictional world he is in. For as its title implies, in terms of its context, content, and key, Barth's big book is indeed defined by and as several species of wordplay, indeed involves the organic and mechanical recombining of letters to deliver a message. Because the key to Barth's work, however, is generated by a process that is the inverse of Bray's ultimate program, involves the replacement of numbers with language, his revolutionary novel initiates and proclaims a second revolution predicated upon an acceptance of "the fact that writing and reading are essentially linear activities,"[10] upon a commitment to print and to an "as if" that may conjure both audience and authority, make possible art, action, and agape, even if it cannot alter the case, make anything happen, or fill in all that is blank.

In detailing his intentions for a book like the one his statements of intention appear in, "The Author" of *LETTERS* suggests that its title is triply significant, referring not only to "epistles" and "the atoms of which the written universe is made" but also "the phenomenon of literature itself" (654). "Having spent the mid-1960's fiddling happily with stories for electronic tape and live voice," he is "inclined now," he writes, "to make the great leap forward again to Print," and since he is an "official honorary Doctor of Letters" who takes "it as among" his "functions to administer artificial resuscitation to the apparently dead," one way he hopes to play that role is by reorchestrating some of the conventions of "that earliest-exhausted of English novel-forms, the *epistolary novel*." The plan he proposes to follow in effecting this entails collecting epistles "from seven correspondents, some recruited from" his "earlier stories," all of which letters are to be "dated over the seven months from March through September 1969, though they may also involve the upcoming U.S. Bicentennial . . . the War of 1812, the American Revolution, revolutions and recyclings generally" (654). All together, these "letters will total 88" and be "divided unequally into seven sections according to a certain scheme" (49).

As the even moderately perceptive reader of *LETTERS* realizes very early on, these statements accurately if incompletely describe the design of the work in progress, *"an old time epistolary novel by seven fictitious drolls & dreamers, each of which imagines himself actual"* (49), five of whom are characters recycled from earlier fictions (Todd Andrews, Jacob Horner, Bray, Ambrose, "The Author"), another a composite character descended from earlier creations (A. B. Cook), and the seventh an entirely new creation (Lady Amherst). Moreover, as the attentive reader also learns rather quickly (particularly if she follows a helpful hint and turns to "Ambrose Mensch's model, postscript to Letter 86" [49]), the schema "The Author" mentions is generated following the rules of an elaborate word game in which a letter or symbol is assigned to each of the book's epistles and placed on a calendar in accordance with the dating of the epistle to spell out at the same time both *LETTERS* and the garrulous subtitle quoted above. Decoding Barth's leafy anagram in this way, we may conclude that the key Ambrose offers to "The Author" is a gift from a "former formalist" (769) that only a practicing one could appreciate, that *LETTERS* is the kind of "complete" and wholly self-referential fiction Bray envisioned.

But, as one suspects Barth knows even if Bray does not, any "formal system" that is "powerful enough" to attain "the capacity for self-reference" must contain "a hole which is tailormade for itself," which "takes the features of the system into account and uses them against the system," dooming it "to incompleteness."[11] Similarly, through self-reference *LETTERS* calls attention to the lacunae in its own scheme, exposes its seams, reveals the imperfections that its Maker, like a Persian artisan, has woven into the design. The 1812 missives of A. B. Cook IV, for example, stretch the rules of the formal game based upon Ambrose's model, while those with which "The Author" formally begins and ends the novel display loose ends and contain blanks. As they attempt to place teller, tale, and told in a temporal context, both of these open letters from "The Author" suggest not only that it is doubtful whether any formal combinatory game can be completely isomorphic with reality and that all truly complex ones must disappear like Burlingame's *Ouida* into their own fundaments, but also that *LETTERS* is an epistle to the reader that will continue to evolve for as long as the literary dialogue takes place in a perpetually protean "now" (42). Every "letter has two times," "The Author" writes in the missive with which "LETTERS is 'now' begun," "that of its writing and that of its reading, which may be so separated, even when the post office does its job, that very little of what obtained when the writer wrote will still when the reader reads. And to the units of epistolary fictions yet a third time is added: the actual date of composition, which will not likely correspond to the letterhead date, a function more of plot or form than of history" (42–44). Although he tries to pinpoint those times, he is, like Tristram Shandy, obliged to keep deferring, for in "the time between" his "first setting down 'March 2, 1969' " on 10/30/73 "and now, 'now' has become January 1974. Nixon won't go away; neither will the 'energy crisis' or inflation-plus-recession or the dreadfulness of nations and their ongoing history." And, "by the time *your* eyes, Reader, review these epistolary fictive *a*'s to *z*'s," he notes, "the 'United States of America' may be setting about its Tri- or Quadricentennial, or be still floundering through its Bi-, or be a mere memory" (45).

Perhaps the most telling example of the book's use of self-reference to suggest its own essential incompleteness and inexhaustibility, however, is the very letter in which Ambrose delivers its design in "A postscript to the Author," thereby seemingly demonstrating that Barth's anonymous minstrel was correct in believing he could be "fertilized . . . as it were with" his "own seed," "messaged" and "inspired" by former versions of his "former self." In the body of that epistle Ambrose transmits what may be taken as another model, presented in the form of an abbreviated alphabet game inspired by his reception of a second water-message consisting "this time wholly of body, without return address, date, salutation, close, or signature" (765). Generated, like his acrostical calendar, out of the initial seven "alphabetical characters," this product of his efforts at "striving through, in order to reach beyond, such games," lists seven entries for each letter, including among them the following: "Alphabetical

Priority, yes: as if to discipline, even if only by artifice, as in formal poetry, our real priorities"; "Dates (of letters) should also 'count': alphabetics + calendrics + serial scansion through seven several correspondents = a form that spells itself while spelling out much more and (one hopes) spellbinding along the way, as language is always also but seldom simply about itself"; "all those locks, and whatever lies beyond them, may be diversions: the real treasure (and our story's resolution) may may be the key itself: illumination, not solution, of the Scheme of Things"; "Fire + algebra = art. Failing the algebra, heartfelt ineptitude; failing the fire, heartless virtuosity" (765–68). To follow this key in decoding Barth's vast "leafy anagram" is to discover that the key to the treasure is indeed the treasure in all of the senses implied by "Dunyazadiad" and that in order to display his heartfelt virtuosity, the "fashioner" of this "funhouse" (766) has devoted as much energy to its plot and plots as to mathematical plotting. The "fiddling" Barth did in "the mid-1960's," we find, not ony failed to obviate his "need to stage his continuing appearance in the world of letters" or to bring back "The Author" for a return engagement in *LETTERS,* but impelled him to redirect his characters through another performance enacted on Clio's stage.

In resurrecting Ambrose and Bray, Todd Andrews and Jacob Horner, and reanimating them to illustrate "the attractions, hazards, rewards, and penalties of a '2nd cycle' isomorphic with the '1st' " (656), and to produce a plot that surges and recedes "like waves of a rising tide," Barth goes back in order to go forward. Filling in lacunae in his characters' previous histories as he updates the uninitiated reader, he fleshes them out so that their life stories may be spun out again to be tied together in a new, if not different, denouement. Revisiting "the Old Line State" (49) to find out where we have all been headed, he rehearses the story of American history as viewed by generations of Cooke's, Cooks, and Burlingames, providing us, as he retraces this genealogy, with documentary evidence that seems to support at least all of the approaches to historiography cataloged by Eben and Henry in *The Sot-Weed Factor.* Apparently completing the loop by making the dates of the letters "count," he brings his characters up to date as well, immersing them in the apocalyptic ambiance of the 1960s, interlocking the historical and the topical, dovetailing the created past with history in the making.

In retelling their tales, the "drolls and dreamers" Barth has redreamed in *LETTERS* follow the patterns of Perseus and Bellerophon, consciously review their personal pasts to see where they are going, only to come to ambiguous or paradoxical conclusions in failing to redeem themselves completely. Todd Andrews, for example, in continuing his interminable inquiries, his unilateral correspondence with his father, remains inclined "on the one hand to see patterns everywhere, on the other to be skeptical of their significance" (255). Becoming half-convinced that his "life has been being recycled since 1954, perhaps since 1937," he "merely" wonders: "If (as Marx says in his essay *The 18th Brumaire*) tragic history repeats itself as farce, what does farce do for an encore?" (256, 255). In effect answering his own question, he goes through a second cycle that is not completely isomorphic with his first, this time around learning "courage" instead of "fear" (257), reliving his affair with Jane Mack not only by resuming his relationship with her but also by engaging in a possibly incestuous liaison with her daughter, and ending up by closing his "Inquiry" and affirming "the Intrinsic Value of Everything, even of Nothingness" (738). Conversely and similarly, Jacob Horner, obsessed by the "Anniversary View of History" but declining *"to rewalk to the end of the road"* (278), finds himself again locking horns with Joe Morgan, who commands that he "Rewrite History," *"Change the Past"* and "Bring Rennie Back to Life" (20). Their roles reversed, their second confrontation ends when Joe, having cuckolded his rival, terminates himself with Jake's assistance, leaving the latter relatively optimistic that he has once more been "Remobilized" and confident that he is ineluctably "Jacob Horner" (744–45).

In spite of the fact that these reenactments contain "as many inversions as repetitions or ironical echoes" (259), however, we are still left contemplating whether "the pans remain balanced for better or worse," whether anyone "in modern terms can tell heads from tails." Todd's final letter suggests that his ultimate stance will involve "turning" his "attention for the last time to" himself (733), and the last testament to his existence is a legal document he composes in a state of almost death, sequestered in a tower awaiting the moment in which he believes he will be blown to pieces. Jake's closing words indicate that he will be taking "the hearse for Wicomico" accompanied by a wife who is only occasionally "Together" (745), and while he may have regained some degree of mobility, Rennie Morgan, of course, has not. *"Sic transit! Plus ça change!"* "The Author" writes in his "Envoi" (772), and just as Barth in redreaming the life stories of Todd and Jake declines to offer either redemption, so too in rewriting

History does he apparently stop short of redeeming either time or the times. Toying with "the role of epistles—real letters, forged and doctored letters—in the history of History" (654) and thereby producing his own doctored version of the past, he leaves us, like Todd, seeing patterns everywhere yet feeling skeptical about their significance. As he retraces the "old line," follows the descendants of Cooke and Burlingame through two centuries of intrigue and counterintrigue, the antithetical aspects of Henry and Eben are translated into a generational conflict that seems to insure that every plot will hatch a counterplot, every revolution be reversed by a counterrevolution. Carrying us from the first American Revolution through the so-called second (the War of 1812), he drops us off amid the clash of culture and counterculture in September of 1969, where we are left to wonder if a conspiracy to detonate the tower containing not only Todd but quite probably several of the book's other dreamers will succeed or fail and if the success or failure of that plot should be read as a sign auguring and characterizing the end of one cycle or the beginning of another. And because Barth refuses to clarify that for us, refuses to indicate outright whether we are to expect a tragic repetition or a farcical encore, an American dream or Dedalian nightmare, even though much of it is about the "bloody business" of history, the only thing his "Bicentennial book"[12] tells us for certain about "capital-H History" (431) is that it "won't go away" (45).

While Barth's novelistic rounding out and updating of former characters might be enough to guarantee that the second cycle of his fiction itself echoes rather than merely repeats or reenacts the first, the key to turning recycling into replenishment in terms of all the book's contexts lies in his introduction of a new variable, his creation of a novel character, Germaine G. Pitt (Lady Amherst). Although most reviewers of *LETTERS* have found her to be the most real and spellbinding of all Barth's creatures, in creating her, he has said, he decided to invert the eighteenth- and nineteenth-century tradition of conceiving of epistolary novels "as *romans à clef*" by challenging himself "to invent a character who bore no resemblance to anyone" he had "ever met in" his "life." A vital product of the wedding of realism and irrealism, Germaine Pitt is indeed, as her name and title suggest, a noble and relevant creation whose fictional existence attests to both her Maker's power to fill in the blank and the historical relationship between British and American cultures. A former "lover or intimate of a number of 'big gun' novelists earlier in the century" who is "cur-

rently marooned in" a "tenth-rate American college,"[13] the passionate
Lady Amherst supplies a good deal of the fire that quickens the alge-
braic universe of Barth's work.

As Max F. Schulz has pointed out in an excellent article that describes LETTERS as a "Great Recombinant American" novel, the
"sorely besieged" damsel of eighteenth-century epistolary novels
"warding off sexual assaults with her left hand while recording them
to a pen pal with the right is transfigured by Barth" into a "fortyish
literary scholar" who "irrepressibly celebrates her dual insatiable sexual and scriblerian appetites," can convey without compunction:
"And yet I hunger and thirst for more: my left hand creeps sleeping-
himward as the right writes on; now I've an instrument in each, poor
swollen darling that I must have again" (70–71).[14] Extending Schulz's
commentary and construction, it might also be said that as Barth
himself writes Lady Amherst into being he assaults and parodies the
genre with his left hand as he renews both it and his art with his
right. Employing all of his modern virtuosity to reexploit the possibilities and work within the extremely limiting conventions of the
epistolary novel, and resuscitating that early-exhausted form by providing a healthy infusion of twentieth-century sexuality, he creates,
moreover, conditions in which past and "present" apparently cross-
fertilize each other.

In accordance with the "Principle of Metaphoric Means," Ambrose,
who is both the lover who inspires Lady Amherst's sexual and literary
excesses and a "capital-A Author" (655) in his own right, is himself
inclined to view Her Ladyship as "a fancied embodiment (among her
other, more human, qualities and characteristics) of the Great Tradition." Having become "infatuated with, enamored of, obsessed by"
her, he "puts her—and himself—through sundry more or less degrad-
ing trials, which she suffers with imperfect love and patience, she being a far from passive lady, until he loses his cynicism and his heart
to her spirited dignity and, at the climax, endeavors desperately,
hopefully, perhaps vainly, to get her one final time with child: his,
hers, theirs" (767). This courtship and the correspondence it leads to
are both the core and source of LETTERS, and in recording them
Barth provides us with a delightful and instructive product and example of his recommitment to linear composition.

Just as the coming together of Ambrose and Lady A., "capital-A
Author" and "Great Tradition," dominates the action when we view

the book as drama, so too do we find that Germaine Pitt's voice becomes dominant when we listen to the virtuoso musical performance Barth executes employing all eighty-eight notes and various keys. Speaking specifically about *LETTERS,* Barth himself has reiterated that he believes his "strong suit" to be "dramaturgy," "that business of creating a 'whole action' in the Aristotelian sense, the awareness that literary works really do have a beginning, middle, and end." Speaking about the genesis of the novel and its musicality, he has indicated that it is in some ways the culmination of years of "experimenting with the ways the human voice could be adapted to forms of written literature" and that in following up his work with tapes and tales orchestrated "within the oral tradition" with an attempt to "orchestrate" the conventions of an essentially linear medium to produce seven believable voices, he hoped to make Lady Amherst's "the sustaining one."[15] Although the affair between Ambrose and Germaine seems to be divided into seven stages as defined "in some oestral almanac of" her "lover's reckoning" (66), and though its future course may therefore turn out to be characterized by recycling or by a series of waning phases that mirror those of its waxing, within the time-span of their letters, their relationship, carrying the rest of the novel with it, surges "forward," recedes, surges "farther forward," recedes "less far, et cetera to its climax and dénouement" (49), completing a plot that is "negentropic" (768). At the same time, if Barth succeeds in sustaining Lady A.'s voice and in making it sustaining, then by departing from past practices such as his evocation of George's dislocating speech, his presentation of the decentered, absent speakers of "Autobiography," "Menelaiad," and "Bellerophoniad," he has used his mastery of the medium and his skills as medium to work through a combinatory playing with sound and create the illusion that the book is filled by an evolving presence.

These two movements reach their mutual climax and commencement in the conclusion of Ambrose's wedding proposal where, as Lady Amherst adds her interpolations to his comments and their two voices are combined, the dominant pronoun becomes "we," the separate monologues a dialogue:

P. S.: Adieu, Art. Now: Will you, dear Germaine, circa 5 P. M. Saturday, 13 September 1969, take me Ambrose as your lawful wedded husband, in dénouements as in climaxes, in sevens as in sixes, till death do us et cet.?

(Pause!

(Hm!

(Well . . .

(I will.   Yes.   I will.) (764–65)

As Schulz has perceptively pointed out, while Barth "delights in toying with the epistemological idea that the motive power of his fiction
draws on the physical laws governing mathematical computations and
computer programming," the real key to *LETTERS* lies in his development of a "parallel biological ontology," and thus "the genetic
coding of the double helix, its continual dividing and recombining of
organisms" both serves as a central "trope for the developmental pattern" of the "lives of the characters" and the form of the book itself,
and draws our attention to "the propaedeutic importance of words not
only to the identity of an individual but also to the recombinative
powers of the writer, and, through him, the vitality and health of the
community."[16] Viewed in the context of such biological emblemizing, the product of the "crossing over" that occurs when Ambrose's
words are wedded to Germaine's can become an "as if" that offers an
alternative to the mechanical, cyclical, or random, for if Lady Amherst's voice is raised for us above the others, her final acceptance of
her lover's proposal ends the book on a note of promise that resonates
with the possibility that future recombinations will lead not to mere
replication or reenactment but to the replenishment of life, language,
and fiction. Establishing a dialogue with the tradition by echoing in
"an old time epistolary novel" the words with which Molly Bloom
concludes Joyce's odyssey, and resounding throughout the multiple
contexts of *LETTERS,* her *"Yes. I will"* may be taken as affirming in
full acknowledgment of limitations that the literary and historical
past may conceivably not only be repeated or parodied in but fecundate the present and future, that the continuous generation and
interaction of "text" and "countertext" (534), revolution and counterrevolution, culture and counterculture may result not in "complex-
ified equilibrium" (767) or utter annihilation but in the evolutionary
"escalation of echoing cycles into ascending spirals" (768).
    This is not to say, of course, that *LETTERS* is free of the satirist's
skepticism, the artificer's delight in the abstract elegance of his own

algebra, or that Barth ceases in this work to erase or cancel with his left hand much of what he inscribes with his right. In tracing the correspondences, we discover that Ambrose has left the "Funhouse" to take up residence in "Menschhaus" and "Lighthouse," bidding a farewell to formalism (768) and responding to "Her" song, filling in the blank of his last name and finding that both he and the water-message are "content," but no matter how much potency he has thereby gained, he may be powerless to prevent his own destruction, may be obliterated on the morrow with Todd and others. Lady Amherst may be pregnant, the consummation of the relationship between "capital-*A* Author" and "fancied embodiment of the Great Tradition" may have propagated a child that is capable of breathing "for itself," is more than "*merely* the product" of the recapitulation of phylogeny (431), but the child, after all, may be Bray's, Ambrose's routing of both the messiah of Numerature and the filmmaker Reg Prinz may represent only the temporary triumph of the "print-oriented bastard." If Barth, however, has managed to synthesize and transcend the antitheses of linearity and disjunction, "naive literary realism" and "Middle-Modernist affectation" (189) to give life to characters who "elicit" our "sympathy,"[17] then we may feel, in summing up, that the gestures of faith outbalance the gestures of cynicism. And if, moreover, the "alphabetical wedding toast" which brings us back to *A* and returns us to the past (770) emblemizes not only the consummation of the lovers' marriage but the author's successful courtship of the reader, then what that faith involves is nothing less than a belief in his effective resuscitation, his restoration to full authority. For, if we are satisfied with what seems to be the case in *LETTERS*, then in revisiting "a certain marsh where once" he "wandered, dozed, and dreamed" (49), the author has employed the limitations and freedom of a Polyeidus to redream the American experience and reexperience the nightmare of history, to embody the "perpetual permutations of the American society" and release the energy generated by its "dynamic openness,"[18] to not only delight us with his combinatory games but instruct us in ethics. Along the way, we might add, he has also managed to learn the trick to the trick that is performed whenever Bach's "Canon per Tonos" is played, has woven the seven voices of *LETTERS*, the separate strands of his seven books, into an "Endlessly Rising Canon,"[19] a "Tangled Hierarchy" that perpetually recycles to its starting point perpetually transformed in order that it may be replayed each time in a new and different key.

Sabbatical

As the nature, emblem, and plot of the book that came after it all imply, the decade of labor that Barth completed and transcended with the publication of *LETTERS* [20] seems to have brought him to a still point, permitted him to arrive at a center and discover a key that obviates, at least temporarily, the need for the outside author, if not "The Author," to pursue future roads to their ends, circle through further labyrinths, or face the fear of paralytic "cosmopsis." Not as impressive in scope and complexity as the "big" work that immediately preceded it, *Sabbatical* probably should be taken as precisely that, as the product of a period of less intense activity following the massive expenditure of creative energy involved in the genesis of Barth's seventh opus. Proferring "the treasure of art, which if it" cannot "redeem the barbarities of history or spare us the horror of living and dying, at least" sustains, refreshes, expands, ennobles, and enriches "our spirits along the painful way" (*Chimera*, 25), it may afford its readers a respite from the pressure of reality. Permitting us to take a temporary leave from our own labors and concerns, it charts the sabbatical voyage of Fenwick Scott Key Turner and his spouse of seven years, Susan Rachel Allan Seckler, a cruise taken while the latter is on sabbatical leave "for the academic year 1979/80," and on which both husband and wife hope to come to "know better" their "hearts and minds vis-à-vis several decisions which lie ahead."[21]

True to its subtitle, *Sabbatical* is also an attempt at reclaiming the romance, at capturing the spirit and conventional images of that mythos and working within the essentially linear form of that genre.[22] Thus, the book exhibits the threefold structure characteristic of many aspects of romance: the book, for example, is divided into three sections or stages labeled "The Cove," "Sailing Up the Chesapeake, Sailing Up the Chesapeake, Sailing Up the Chesapeake Bay," and "The Fork"; its regnant visual image is that of three waterways, passages, or courses of action meeting in a point; like many of Barth's works it is informed by a biological conceit, in this case two eggs traveling down the two fallopian tubes on their way toward encountering a spermatozoon.[23] Once again as well, Barth draws upon the pattern of quest and the quest to relate the quest, but the fictional universe of *Sabbatical* is not nearly as temporally or spatially displaced as those of *The Sot-Weed Factor* or *Giles Goat-Boy,* and in it the central conflict between opposites, between the forces of light and darkness, takes place in a setting very much akin to our own world, the quotidian realm W. H. Auden called "middle earth." In deference to tradition, however, the tale is sprinkled with conventional water images, including a contemporary avatar of leviathan, a sea-monster out of Jules Verne affectionately named "Chessie," and the narrative contains many other examples of the marvelous and mysterious, such as the seemingly miraculous return of Fenn's lost boina, the discovery of an ominous island that does not appear on the charts, several possibly inexplicable disappearances, a series of perhaps significant coincidences, an instance of discovery or "extraordinary illumination" (355), and episodes that apparently attest to the prognosticative power of naming and the puzzling influence of ancestry (Fenn is allegedly a descendant of Francis Scott Key, Susan of Edgar Allan Poe). Finally, playing upon the analogies between the quest-romance and both dreams and ritual, *Sabbatical* not only suggests at times that it be viewed as a five-part dream vision containing shared dreams as well as dreamed "flashbacks" and "flashforwards," but also manifests the triumph of fertility over the sterility of the waste land.

It is through exploiting in particular these latter conventional aspects of the pattern that Barth most effectively achieves the kind of fusion of the fanciful and irreal with the topical and realistic he called for in "The Literature of Replenishment," for in *Sabbatical,* as in many traditional romances, the sterility in question is not only natural but social, and the wish-fulfillment dream, the desire for self-fulfillment and communal reintegration often descends into the elegiac or into moody brooding and threatens at times to become an anxiety dream. The protected microcosm Fenn and Susan have made for themselves and created for us in composing their life story is assaulted at every point on its circumference by the destructive forces of contemporary society and weakened at its center by self-doubt and indecision.

We are, for instance, persistently reminded of Fenwick's former association with the Central Intelligence Agency, something that remains for him a source of guilt, fear, and uncertainty as he recalls his at least peripheral involvement in past crimes and contemplates the possibly fatal forms of retaliation the exposé he has published may provoke. Susan's "younger half-brother," Gus, we learn, was presumably tortured and murdered in Chile "where he had gone in 1973 to help oppose the CIA's successful efforts to 'destabilize' the socialist government of the late President Salvador Allende Gossens" (32–33);

her mother, Carmen, a "girlhood survivor of the earliest Nazi concentration camps," has gone "kerflooey" (28); her twin sister, Miriam, has the dubious distinction of being "perhaps the only U.S. citizen" to have been imprisoned and tortured with electrical devices by SAVAK, the Shah of Iran's secret police (27). In a ten-page passage that recalls in its excruciating realism the account of Rennie's death in *The End of the Road,* Susan mercilessly relates *"THE STORY OF MIRIAM'S OTHER RAPES."* Describing the degradation and physical and mental abuse her sister was made to suffer at the hands of a motorcycle gang, a psychotic "redneck," and a passing motorist, she manages to convince us that while "Rape and Torture and Terror are just words," "the details are what's real" (66).

In numerous places Fenn and Sue must modify their narrative design, distort the shape of their fiction to accommodate what is the case. The footnotes that they supply supposedly for the benefit of the reader begin to tell their own tale, attesting, like actuarial tables, to the world's arbitrariness and finality: "Jack Seckler died in 1949 at age 31 when the Cadillac he was driving, alone, back to his and Carmen's then house in Cheltenham, Pa., from a visit to his mother Havah in Pikesville, Md., was struck head-on along Route 40 by a tractor-trailer loaded with live Leghorn chickens, whose driver dozed off at 60 mph east of Elkton, exactly on the Maryland/Delaware state line" (170). Intrigued by the similarities between his mysterious disappearance and that of Fenwick's twin brother Manfred, "Prince of Darkness," also a CIA operative, the joint narrators present *"THE STRANGE TRUE CASE OF JOHN ARTHUR PAISLEY"* by providing twenty pages worth of excerpts taken from the *Baltimore Sun* (1978–80), shifting from romance to reportage, temporarily turning their fanciful sea story into a collection of actual documents.

Succumbing to the "diffused, resigned, melancholy sense of the passing of time" that is to be found in romances such as Tennyson's *Passing of Arthur,*[24] Fenwick and Susan find that the "world's regressing like crazy" and wonder whether it can be true that it is "going back to go forward" (285). Having sailed out and oceanward and circled back to retrace their way up the Chesapeake, and having failed on their sabbatical voyage to resolve, as they had intended, many of the major questions confronting them, they are also distressed by the possibility that their life story is following a comparable course. Uncertain about whether he should attempt to become a "real" writer, he is troubled as well by a heart condition that makes him painfully aware of "what William James called the pinch of one's personal destiny as it spins itself out upon the wheel" (221). Doubting her own vocation, unsure about whether her responsibility is to educate the elite or serve the masses, she, like he, experiences a dark night in which she faces the menace of potential futures, dreams of "the physical collapse" of the entire universe, envisions "a black hole aspirating, with a cosmic shlup, us, U.S., all" (321). Creating what is perhaps the most powerful image of sterility in the book, she takes us through the mechanical abortion of the twin foetuses she and Fenwick had brought to life during their voyage, an action apparently motivated by her indecision, her confusion about her husband's true wishes, and a more generalized insecurity about the state of things.

In spite of the fact, however, that *Sabbatical* is thus affected perhaps more than any of Barth's other books by the pressures of contemporary existence, we may still be led to conclude that the goals of the quest-romance have to an extent been achieved, that the desire "for a fulfillment that will" both "deliver" us "from the anxieties of reality" and "contain that reality" has been satisfied, that an "integrated body," whether "individual or social, or both," has been successfully "defended."[25] After all of their soul-searching, Fenwick and Susan determine to "swing with the tides and winds, take what comes," "do" their "work" and "savor" their "pleasures and each other, while" they "may," offering what little they can to the world, and hoping for "the best" (360). Although they may never have children, they come to share the satisfaction Fenn feels whenever he marvels at the fact that "anything should live, grow, evolve, reflect, respond to beauty, reproduce its kind . . . or make further beauty of another kind." Unable to dispel their nostalgia for what might have been or their apprehension about what yet may come to be, they nevertheless decide that the fragile, insulated realm they have created is worth preserving, that if "art," "learning and civilization" are not "enough," they are at least "far better than nothing" (362–63). Having arrived at a fork in the twin channels of their life together and their joint narrative, they discover that "at a place where three roads meet, there are four choices" (351), resolve to remain in terms of perspective "right at the fork; right at the hub" (359), finding there a kind of fertility. Fertilized by the past, messaged by Poe's *Narrative of Arthur Gordon Pym*, they realize that the life story they have brought into existence is their offspring, that the "doing and the telling," their "writing" and their "loving" are "twins," that even though they, like

Pym, may be swept toward the South Polar abyss at the vernal equinox, since they are still "near the solstice," there is time for them yet. The point of their story they learn "is that the point of Poe's story is that the point of Pym's story is this: 'It is not that the end of the voyage interrupts the writing, but that the interruption of the writing ends the voyage' " (365, 362).

In order to emblemize not only this resolution but other aspects of the book, Barth has placed on the title page of *Sabbatical* a design consisting of an open-ended *Y* incompletely contained by a circle and containing at its fork another circle. Resembling a steering wheel, this emblem is suggestive not only of destiny but of the sterile and mechanical, the "shlups" of the vacuum aspirator that sucks the life out of Susan's womb, of the "Black Hole" that threatens to swallow up her, Pym, all. Viewed from a different perspective, however, it becomes a diagram of the female reproductive system, a depiction of the book's basic biological conceit that focuses our attention on the point of conception, reminds us of the rejuvenative potential of nature, the power of the artist to fecundate the twin ova of fact and fancy within the protected microcosm of his fiction. Taken, lastly, as both a schematic representing the relationship between teller, tale and told, and a chart recording the course of Barth's career it may be interpreted as affirming the aesthetic outlined in "The Literature of Replenishment" while implying that Barth himself has resolved to remain at the hub, "right at the fork" where are met the twin channels leading forward "toward Italo Calvino and Gabriel García Márquez" and back "to Aristotle by way of" "Nabokov's posthumous *Lectures on Literature*" (232).

Indeed, to a much greater extent than *LETTERS, Sabbatical* functions as "a loving, sportive sally between the 'truly wed' " (272), reflecting throughout its design the attitude that storytelling and lovemaking are twins. The book's superficial simplicity, its use of foreshadowing, explanatory footnotes, digressions, and asides, seem to be intended not to deceive or mock the innocent reader, but to entice, coax, and guide her. Like a masterfully composed luc-bát (a form of Vietnamese poetry practiced by Miriam's mate "Eastward Ho"), Barth's romance substitutes "delicacy" for "obscurity," relies on a kind of connotative resonance and displays a kind of formal intricacy that can be savored by anyone familiar with the general cultural context and capable of putting "two and two together" (272). At the same time, the author has not forgotten the reader whose long-term fidelity he has won. For the initiated reader who has followed him through the "Funhouse," Barth's purposeful use of relatively obvious devices, such as the essential pretense that Fenwick and Susan are composing their story as they live it and we read it, may in itself hold a certain significance. Moreover, by adhering to his practice of weaving motifs and phrases from his previous works into the composition, Barth makes this comparatively simple tune reverberate for those familiar with his fiction as a whole.

While both *Sabbatical* and *LETTERS*, then, may be characterized as accomplished products of the rehearsals effected and the promises made in *Chimera*, the former is by nature a much less ambitious book, and of the two, therefore, it is the latter that is much more likely to contribute over the course of time to the augmentation of Barth's reputation. For *LETTERS* is not only a "big" book that rivals Barth's other "big" books but an American novel that aspires to a place in the pantheon of grand American novels. Combining the satirist's distrust of systems and commitment to exposing human weakness and folly with the artificer's enjoyment of patterns and the realist's affinity for character, it seeks to provoke not only an aesthetic but an emotional response, endeavors to address not only "the facts of life" but also "its conditions." Both encyclopedic and authoritative, it successfully synthesizes antitheses and validates Barth's program for a literature of replenishment every bit as effectively as *One Hundred Years of Solitude, Cosmicomics*, or just about any other major work of fiction published in the last two or three decades.

Chapter Nine
Unwritable Postscript, Ironical Coda

As he awaits the "unwritable postscript" to his "*Anonymiad*," Barth's stranded bard acknowledges that there can be "no dénouement" to his "Last Lay," "only a termination or ironical coda." Similarly, if for different reasons, any study of Barth's oeuvre must at this point in time end inconclusively, close with the admission that there is much that necessarily has been "left unsaid," much that, for now at least, "must be blank" (*Funhouse*, 193). For Barth lives and writes on, remains engaged in the construction of his floating opera. Somewhere "past the middle" of his creative life, he has given us every reason to suspect that he will continue to launch his own message-laden amphorae, committed, as always, to perfecting the craft of storytelling, buoyed by the conceptions of audience and authority that inform *LETTERS* and *Sabbatical*, and motivated by a resolution to fashion a second cycle of works that are truly different from those of the first, that not only delight but instruct, that are "not only passionately formal, not only passionately 'in the language,' as Theodore Roethke used to say about poems he liked, but passionately about things in life as well."[1] At present, Barth's "significance," his place in the tradition remain, of course, matters very much under consideration or open to debate. His work still draws a good deal of critical attention, and while there are those who, as always, are of the opinion that he has reduced the art of fiction to the chronicling "of minstrel misery," there are also many who are willing to affirm that he has added a number of "minstrel masterpieces" ("Anonymiad," 193) to the treasury.

In reviewing the first three decades of Barth's career in order to abstract its course and arrive at a provisional assessment of his contribution, it may be useful to once again create an historical context by focusing on the apparent distinctions between modernist and postmodernist attitudes toward language, order, and identity. Attempting to spell out a formula without resorting to "the technical language of the structuralists," Jerome Mazzaro has proposed that

"the essential differences between 'modernism' and 'postmodernism' "
may be briefly and broadly outlined as follows: "in conceiving of language as a fall from unity, modernism seeks to restore the original
state often by proposing silence or the destruction of language; postmodernism accepts the division and uses language and self-definition—much as Descartes interpreted thinking—as the basis of
identity. Modernism tends, as a consequence, to be more mystical in
the traditional senses of that word whereas postmodernism, for all its
seeming mysticism, is irrevocably worldly and social."[2] While Mazzaro introduced this formulation to facilitate a discussion of the nature of postmodern American poetry, and while we must also keep in
mind Barth's assertion that the "particular work ought always to take
primacy over contexts and categories,"[3] we may nonetheless notice a
certain resonance between Mazzaro's description of what he believes
to be an historical development and some of Barth's accounts of the
evolution of his fiction.

In rehearsing the story of his stories for the benefit of John
Hawkes, Barth, for instance, is reported to have said the following:

I have at times gone farther than I want to go in the direction of a fiction
that foregrounds language and form, displacing the ordinary notion of content, of "aboutness." But beginning with the "Chimera" novellas—written
after the "Lost in the Funhouse" series, where that foregrounding reaches its
peak or its nadir, depending on your esthetic—I have wanted my stories to
be *about* things: about the passions, which Aristotle tells us are the true subject of literature. I'm with Aristotle on that. Of course form can be passionate; language itself can be passionate. These are not the passions of the
viscera, but that doesn't give them second-class citizenship in the republic of
the passions. More and more, as I get older, I nod my head yes to Aristotle.[4]

If we wish to perform such a reductive operation, we may distill
Barth's remarks to produce a pattern that seems to fit Mazzaro's formulation and to suggest that the ontogeny of his fiction as a whole
has been characterized by a general shift from a preoccupation with
the modernist sensibility to a seemingly wholehearted celebration of
the postmodernist position as Mazzaro defines them.

Thus, if we recapitulate the overtly expressed or regnant attitudes
toward language to be found in each of Barth's books, we may indeed
note that in the first five the increasing predominance of the kind of
linguistic and formal foregrounding of which he has spoken is causally

related to, or associated with, a sense of disunity or disjunction, a
sometimes nearly paralytic concern about the gap between word and
world, verbal imitation and thought or action. Both *The Floating Opera* and *The End of the Road*, for example, expend a good part of their
energy in blunting the diagnostic and graphic implements of the literary realist, thereby driving a wedge into the crack between the
Jamesian rendered surface and the meaning or essence of things.
Moreover, as the reader will recall, Todd's verbal gamesmanship and
his insistence on the "vagrant" nature of his prose and Jake's verbal
connoisseurship and his assertion of the inadequacy of naming become
related on the one hand to an obsession with "the gap between fact
and opinion," and on the other to the perception that the self is "discontinuous." Todd, of course, ends up secure in his "ultimate irresponsibility," having dislocated himself from any ethical context and
freed himself from the arbitrariness of personality, while Jake, at the
conclusion of the book's plot, ends up "terminal," holding a dead instrument in his hands, having brought about the severance of all possible dialogues, their isolation and apprehension of disjunction
anticipating Eben's innocence and fall and the Goat-Boy's "unspeakable" knowledge and inability to communicate. Dominated by Eben's
notion that "the sound of Mother English" is "more fun to game with
than her sense to labor over" and by George's eclectic and dislocating
voice, both *The Sot-Weed Factor* and *Giles Goat-Boy* "foreground" verbal play at the same time that they displace "the ordinary notion"
of "aboutness" by burlesquing the encyclopedic tendencies of realism,
lampooning the mythic and the allegorical. The apparent emphasis on
linguistic opacity and on puns, patterns, and patterning in Barth's
third and fourth works becomes as he has suggested perhaps even
more pronounced in *Lost in the Funhouse*, a book that he himself has
labeled as "mainly late-modernist,"[5] and which presents us with myr-
iad reflective surfaces and echo chambers, with numerous "selves,"
stranded speakers, caught in a state of arrested development or frac-
tional existence, with combinatory games played in counterpoint to
the biological conceits that run through the series as a whole.

Some critics and reviewers, taking *Lost in the Funhouse* as Barth's
consummate statement, and reading it as a kind of straightforward
endorsement and emulation of the strategies and sensibilities of Beckett and Borges, have asserted or intimated that Barth continues to
write out of sheer perversity or persistence, that having reconciled
himself to practicing a species of formalism devoid of any intrinsic

value, he goes on simply to go on, awaiting the "unwritable postscript" to his oeuvre, approaching the terminus at which he will
finally "cap his pen" or where his ultimate farewell performance will
trail off into silence. Not only do such evaluations, however, ignore
the tone of many of the pieces in the "Funhouse" series, fail to consider the possibility that Barth's treatment of the modernist program
and geist may be at least a trifle disingenuous if not in fact parodic,
but they also do not account for Barth's suggestion that beginning
with *Chimera* he effected a shift in emphasis, fine-tuned his aesthetic
and became less concerned with the effort to foreground language and
form that reached "its peak or nadir" in his "fiction for print, tape,
live voice." Indeed, as we have seen, commencing with his novella
sequence, Barth, while still calling our attention to division, still
making us aware that language and form can be passionate in and of
themselves, began to accentuate the possibility of reestablishing a re-
unifying dialogue, began reemphasizing the conception of writing as
procreative act, reasserting the authority he had dispersed in *Giles* and
Lost in the Funhouse. Restating the key to this turn, the "as if" of
"Dunyazadiad" that balances out the ironic apotheosis of "Perseid"
and the Bellerophonic betrayals and Polyeidic flux of "Bellerophoniad," "The Author" of *LETTERS* instructs Ambrose: "Never mind
what your predecessors have come up with, and never mind that in a
sense this 'dialogue' is a monologue; that we capital-*A* Authors are
ultimately, ineluctably, and forever talking to ourselves. If our correspondence is after all a fiction, we like, we *need* that fiction: it makes
our job less lonely" (655). If *we* feel that in *LETTERS* and *Sabbatical*
voice has again become a locus and medium of personality, it may be
because those books make even greater claims than "The Author"
does, imply that the need of which he writes is not only an individual
one but a communal one, that in accepting division and using "language and self-definition as the basis of identity," the writer may be
able to perform the same service for his culture that he performs for
himself.

As Schulz has perceptively put it, in his later fiction Barth seeks
to acknowledge the modernist concern with derangement and division, "with the indeterminacy of signs, signifier, and signified" and
"to merge these verbal contingencies with a fictional world of defin-
able peoples, places, and times."[6] Although Barth's work has been
judged in the past to contain elements of mysticism, even in earlier
books such as *Giles Goat-Boy*, whatever mysteries are alluded to are

"unspeakable," by nature inexpressible, and the mystical impulse is countered by satyric acceptance and revelry, by a profound awareness of death and limitation. In any case, *LETTERS* and *Sabbatical* blend the irreal with a good portion of what is "irrevocably worldly and social," deal, as Barth has pointed out "with something like contemporary problems among contemporary people—people whom" the author wishes "to be believable."[7] In these novels, metaphysical mystery has given way to the wonderful, to the kind of magic practiced by an artist functioning not as a priest but as an enchanter.

Given all of this, there is a certain irony to the fact that the works which have so far won Barth the greatest and widest degree of public response are those that are most clearly characterized by linguistic and formal foregrounding, and that have been therefore deemed by more than one less than astute reviewer to be unintelligible or pointless. While *The Sot-Weed Factor, Giles Goat-Boy,* and *Lost in the Funhouse* have earned Barth an undeniable place in literary history and placed him, in the eyes of at least a few critics, on an equal footing with the exemplars he pays homage to in "The Literature of Exhaustion," one gets the feeling that, at least for the time being, Barth would rather keep permanent company with Calvino and Márquez, would like to be remembered as a progenitor and exemplary master of "the best next thing" after modernism. Since "Fame's a fickle Slut, and whory," to insure that reputation, it is likely that he will have to follow up the remarkable achievement of *LETTERS*, guided by the program of synthesis or transcension outlined in "The Literature of Replenishment." If it is far too early to tell how well Barth's fiction will wear, what can be predicted with a good deal more certainty is that he will continue to aspire to become a Dickens or Twain or Cervantes, will persist in striving to produce ambitious and substantive works, engaging stories, and to continuously ground and renew his art by returning to his origins and cultivating a sense of place—his ninth book, he has indicated, will be a "longish" one; its working title is *The Tidewater Tales: A Novel.*[8] Remembering, however, that "there's no future for prophets" and that Barth considers critical categories and schemata, such as the ones proposed above, to be "as more or less fishy as they are less or more useful," it is perhaps best to conclude not with further prognostications or attempts at reaching a denouement, but with a coda, offering as such Douglas Hofstadter's description of Bach's marvelous and ingenious *Musical Offering*, a description that by significant coincidence also fits Barth's own compositions in a not wholly different medium:[9] "Things are going on on many levels . . . There are tricks with notes and letters; there are ingenious variations on the King's Theme; there are original kinds of canons; there are extraordinarily complex fugues; there is beauty and extreme depth of emotion; even an exultation in the many-leveledness of the work comes through."

Notes and References

Chapter One

1. Charlie Reilly, "An Interview with John Barth," *Contemporary Literature* 22, no. 1 (1981):8.
2. Ibid., 23.
3. "The Literature of Replenishment: Postmodernist Fiction," *Atlantic* 245, no. 1 (1980):69. To sample some of the attempts to label Barth, see Robert Scholes, *The Fabulators* (New York, 1967); Charles B. Harris, *Contemporary Novelists of the Absurd* (New Haven, 1971); John W. Tilton, *Cosmic Satire in the Contemporary Novel* (Lewisburg, 1977); John Stark, *The Literature of Exhaustion: Borges, Nabokov, Barth* (Durham, N. C., 1974).
4. "Muse, Spare Me," *Book Week*, 26 September 1965, 28–29.
5. See Alan Prince, "An Interview with John Barth," *Prism* (Sir George Williams University), Spring 1968, 45, and Arthur Cooper, "An In-Depth Interview with John Barth," *Harrisburg Patriot*, 30 March 1965, 6.
6. Prince, "Interview," 49.
7. Ibid., 44. For a more complete biographical sketch, see David Morrell, *John Barth: An Introduction* (University Park, 1976), 121–31.
8. "Landscape: The Eastern Shore," *Kenyon Review* 22, no. 1 (1960):106.
9. See Morrell, *John Barth*, 126–27.
10. John Enck, "John Barth: An Interview," *Wisconsin Studies in Contemporary Literature* 6 (Winter–Spring 1965):7.
11. Prince, "Interview," 50.
12. Interview by Joe David Bellamy in *The New Fiction: Interviews with Innovative American Writers* (Urbana, 1974), 16.
13. See Morrell, *John Barth*, 123.
14. See Prince, "Interview," 45; Bellamy, *New Fiction*, 14.
15. James McKenzie, "Pole-Vaulting in Top Hats: A Public Conversation with John Barth, William Gass, and Ishmael Reed," *Modern Fiction Studies* 22, no. 2 (1976):138.
16. Prince, "Interview," 45–46.
17. Enck, "John Barth," 9–10.
18. Richard Ellmann, *James Joyce* (New York: Oxford University Press, 1982), 703.
19. "The Literature of Replenishment," 70.
20. Ellmann, *James Joyce*, 703.
21. Bellamy, *New Fiction*, 12; Barth, "The Literature of Replenishment," 69.

22. "Muse, Spare Me," 28 and afterword to *The Adventures of Roderick Random*, by Tobias Smollett (New York, 1964), 479.

23. "The Literature of Exhaustion," *Atlantic* 220, no. 2 (1967):29–34; quotations in this and the subsequent two paragraphs are from this source.

24. Quotations in this and the subsequent two paragraphs are from "The Literature of Replenishment," 65–71.

25. Robert Scholes, "George Is My Name," *New York Times Book Review*, 7 August 1966, 1.

Chapter Two

1. John Barth, *The Floating Opera* (New York, 1981), p. 246; hereafter cited in the text. I have chosen to work with this later version of the book, rather than with the 1956 Appleton, Century Crofts edition, because Barth has indicated that he bowdlerized the earlier version to please the publisher and that it does not represent his true intentions.

2. *The End of the Road* (New York, 1981), 198; hereafter cited in the text; this is identical with the revised 1967 Doubleday version.

3. Barth to David Morrell, 5 November 1969, quoted in Morrell's *John Barth*, 13; John Enck, "John Barth," 10–11.

4. Barth himself has alluded to the similarities between *The Floating Opera* and *Tristram Shandy*. See, for example, Prince, "Interview," 47. In comparing Barth's novels with such Menippean satires, I am following the lead of others. For a brief summary of what they have said, see Charles B. Harris, "John Barth and the Critics: An Overview," in *Critical Essays on John Barth*, ed. Joseph W. Waldmeir (Boston, 1980), 10–11.

5. Enck, "John Barth," 8.

6. Ibid.

7. Barth has indicated that he received his Sterne via Machado. See, for example, Prince, "Interview," 47 and Enck, "John Barth," 3–4.

Chapter Three

1. George Bluestone, "John Wain and John Barth: The Angry and the Accurate," *Massachusetts Review* 1 (May 1960):586; quoted in Morrell, *John Barth*, 16.

2. Prince, "Interview," 55–56.

3. David Kerner, "Psychodrama in Eden," *Chicago Review* 13 (Winter–Spring 1959):59–67; reprinted in *Critical Essays on John Barth*, ed. Joseph J. Waldmeir, 94.

4. Morrell, *John Barth*, 25.

5. Prince, "Interview," 57.

6. Northrop Frye, *Anatomy of Criticism: Four Essays* (Princeton: Princeton University Press, 1971), 231. I employ Frye's definitions of satire and anatomy throughout this study.

7. Enck, "John Barth," 11.
8. See Prince, "Interview," 54.
9. Max Black, *A Companion to Wittgenstein's "Tractatus"* (Ithaca, N.Y.: Cornell University Press, 1964), 8, 11, 14. My remarks on Wittgenstein here are generally dependent upon Black's commentary. For more on Barth and Wittgenstein, see Tony Tanner, *City of Words* (New York, 1971), 230–59.
10. Ludwig Wittgenstein, *Tractatus Logico-Philosophicus*, trans. D. F. Pears and B. F. McGuinness (London: Routledge & Kegan Paul, 1961), 147, 151.
11. Prince, "Interview," 58.
12. Ibid.

Chapter Four

1. Enck, "John Barth," 4. Barth, of course, not only eventually read but also wrote about that "Hindu thing." See his essay *"The Ocean of Story,"* in *Directions in Literary Criticism: Contemporary Approaches to Literature*, ed. Stanley Weintraub and Philip Young (University Park, 1973), 1–6.
2. McKenzie, "Pole-Vaulting," 136–37. Actually, Barth probably picked up the phrase "the secret adventures of order" from Jorge Luis Borges. See Borges's essay "Valéry as Symbol" in his *Other Inquisitions 1937–1952*, trans. Ruth L. C. Simms (New York: Simon & Schuster, 1965), 74.
3. Frye, *Anatomy*, 224.
4. McKenzie, "Pole-Vaulting," 137.
5. Enck, "John Barth," 13.
6. Prince, "Interview," 48.
7. Ibid., 49.
8. Ibid., 48.
9. *The Sot-Weed Factor* (New York, 1969), 9; hereafter cited in the text; this is identical with the revised 1967 Doubleday second edition.
10. Hugh Kenner, *The Stoic Comedians* (Berkeley: University of California Press, 1962), 54–55. Both this and the preceding paragraph draw upon Kenner's study of Flaubert, Joyce, and Beckett.
11. "The Literature of Replenishment," 71.
12. Prince, "Interview," 45.
13. Ian Watt, introduction to *The Life and Opinions of Tristram Shandy, Gentleman*, by Laurence Sterne (Boston: Houghton Mifflin, 1965), xx–xxvii. Italics mine.
14. Ibid., xx–xxi.
15. See, for example, Morrell, *John Barth*, 27–48 and Philip E. Diser, "The Historical Ebenezer Cooke," *Critique* 10 (1968):48–59.
16. Prince, "Interview," 50–51.
17. Several critics have written well on Barth's use of the Adamic myth in the book. See, for example, Jac Tharpe, *John Barth: The Comic Sublimity of*

Paradox (Carbondale, 1974), 34–51, and Manfred Puetz, "*The Sot-Weed Factor*: The Pitfalls of Mythopoesis," *Twentieth Century Literature* 22 (1976):454–66, reprinted in *Critical Essays on John Barth*, ed. Waldmeir, 134–45.
18. Prince, "Interview," 56.
19. Watt, "Introduction," xviii.
20. Prince, "Interview," 58.
21. Ibid., 57.
22. Enck, "John Barth," 7.

Chapter Five

1. James T. Gresham has explored at length the affinities between *Giles* and other Menippean satires. See his essay "*Giles Goat-Boy*: Satyr, Satire, and Tragedy Twined," *Genre* 7, no. 2 (1974):148–63; reprinted in *Critical Essays on John Barth*, ed. Waldmeir, 157–71.
2. Frye, *Anatomy*, 90.
3. Enck, "John Barth," 8; Prince, "Interview," 46.
4. Prince, "Interview," 59.
5. Ibid., 46, 48; McKenzie, "Pole-Vaulting," 151.
6. *Giles Goat-Boy or, The Revised New Syllabus* (New York, 1981), 41; hereafter cited in the text.
7. See Morrell, *John Barth*, 60, 71–73 on Barth's use of Campbell's work.
8. Joseph Campbell, *The Hero with a Thousand Faces* (Princeton: Princeton University Press, 1968), 347, 40, 257.
9. Frye, *Anatomy*, 54–60, 315.
10. Prince, "Interview," 59; Enck, "John Barth," 12.
11. Barth, lecture delivered to the Pennsylvania State University faculty, 13 July 1965; quoted in Morrell, *John Barth*, 66.
12. McKenzie, "Pole-Vaulting," 151.
13. "Heroic Comedy," *Newsweek*, 8 August 1966, 82.
14. Campbell, *Hero*, 29.
15. Frye, *Anatomy*, 235–36.
16. See ibid., 314, on *Finnegans Wake*, and Scott Byrd, "*Giles Goat-Boy* Visited," *Critique: Studies in Modern Fiction* 9, no. 1 (1966):108–112.
17. Prince, "Interview," 62, 58–59.
18. Frye, *Anatomy*, 212.
19. Gresham, "*Giles Goat-Boy*," 168; Gerhard Joseph, *John Barth*, University of Minnesota Pamphlets on American Writers, no. 91 (Minneapolis, 1970), 36.
20. Gresham, "*Giles Goat-Boy*," 169; Scholes, *The Fabulators*, 167.
21. Campbell, *Hero*, 147.
22. Ibid., 137.
23. See Frye, *Anatomy*, 54.

24. Ibid., 213.
25. Quoted by Joseph J. Waldmeir in his review of *Giles Goat-Boy*; reprinted in *Critical Essays on John Barth*, ed. Waldmeir, 156n.
26. Gresham, *"Giles Goat-Boy,"* 157–58.
27. Frye, *Anatomy*, 323–24; William Carlos Williams, *Paterson* (New York: New Directions, 1963), 239.

Chapter Six

1. Bellamy, *New Fiction*, 8.
2. *Lost in the Funhouse: Fiction for Print, Tape, Live Voice* (New York, 1969), ix; hereafter cited in the text; this edition contains all of the author's notes Barth has written.
3. Bellamy, *New Fiction*, 8–9.
4. *Chimera* (New York, 1973), 320; hereafter cited in the text.
5. McKenzie, "Pole-Vaulting," 137. For a discussion of Barth's use of "Chinese boxes" see Stark, *Literature of Exhaustion*, 124–25.
6. McKenzie, "Pole-Vaulting," 141. Charles Caramello has also linked "Frame-Tale," Scheherazade, and death. See the section on Barth in his *Silverless Mirrors: Book, Self & Postmodern American Fiction* (Tallahassee, 1983), 112–21.
7. "The Literature of Exhaustion," 33; Jorge Luis Borges, "Partial Enchantments of the *Quixote*," in *Other Inquisitions*, 45.
8. Borges, "Partial Enchantments," 46.
9. Douglas R. Hofstadter, *Gödel, Escher, Bach: An Eternal Golden Braid* (New York: Vintage, 1980), 10, 15. One reviewer has compared Hofstadter's book to Barth's *LETTERS*; see Gary Thompson, "Barth's Letters and Hawkes' Passion," *Michigan Quarterly Review* 19, no. 2 (1980):270.
10. "The Literature of Exhaustion," 33; Hofstadter, *Gödel*, 15. For an extensive examination of the role of paradox in Barth's fiction, see Tharpe, *John Barth*.
11. See Hofstadter, *Gödel*, 686–92, for an explanation of how every system contains a "protected" or "inviolate" level, "unassailable by the rules on other levels, no matter how tangled their interaction may be among themselves."
12. Sterne, *Tristram Shandy*, 4–5.
13. For a description of some of the forms of the mythic "night-sea journey," see, for example, Erich Neumann, *The Great Mother: An Analysis of the Archetype* (Princeton: Princeton University Press, 1972), 157–58, 177.
14. See Borges, "On the Cult of Books," in *Other Inquisitions*, 117. Borges, of course, quotes the *Timaeus*.
15. See Morrell, *John Barth*, 88–89.
16. Borges, "On the Cult of Books," 117–18.

17. Herman Melville, *Moby-Dick; or, The Whale* (New York: W. W. Norton, 1967), 84, 399, 83.

18. Ibid., 399.

19. Borges, "On the Cult of Books," 120.

20. Borges, "Avatars of the Tortoise," in *Other Inquisitions*, 114.

21. My discussion of the Escher lithograph draws upon the analysis by Hofstadter, *Gödel*, 689–90.

22. For further speculation on Barth's response to Joyce's work, see Michael Hinden, *"Lost in the Funhouse*: Barth's Use of the Recent Past," *Twentieth Century Literature* 19, no. 2 (1973):107–18; reprinted in *Critical Essays on John Barth*, ed. Waldmeir, 190–200.

23. Borges, "Avatars of the Tortoise," 114.

24. Hofstadter, *Gödel*, 688–89.

25. See "The Literature of Exhaustion," 34.

26. Ibid.; Borges's "Histriones," he notes, are a heretical sect "who believe that repetition is impossible in history and therefore live viciously in order to purge the future of the vices they commit." Shakespeare's "heroic metamorphoses," according to Borges, won him a conversation with God. See Jorge Luis Borges, "Everything and Nothing," in *A Personal Anthology*, ed. Anthony Kerrigan (New York: Grove Press, 1967), 115–17.

27. "The Literature of Exhaustion," 34.

28. Borges, "From Someone to No One," in *A Personal Anthology*, 120–21.

Chapter Seven

1. McKenzie, "Pole-Vaulting," 151.

2. Hofstadter, *Gödel*, 135–36, 152.

3. McKenzie, "Pole-Vaulting," 136–37.

4. Bellamy, *New Fiction*, 12.

5. The quotation is from Caramello, *Silverless Mirrors*, 118–19. See also Edward Said, "Contemporary Fiction and Criticism," *TriQuarterly*, no. 33 (1975):237.

6. For a more complete analysis of the narrative design of each novella, see Cynthia Davis, " 'The Key to the Treasure': Narrative Movements and Effects in *Chimera*," *Journal of Narrative Technique* 5, no. 2 (1975):105–15; reprinted in Waldmeir, ed., *Critical Essays on John Barth*, 217–27.

7. McKenzie, "Pole-Vaulting," 137–38.

8. See Morrell, *John Barth*, 162.

9. Borges, "For Bernard Shaw," in *Other Inquisitions*, 163.

Chapter Eight

1. "The Literature of Exhaustion," 29–30, 32.

2. Caramello, *Silverless Mirrors*, 116.

3. Ibid., 116, 121.

4. Reilly, "Interview," 11.

5. "The Literature of Replenishment," 69.

6. Reilly, "Interview," 12.

7. Borges, "For Bernard Shaw," 163, 166.

8. "The Literature of Replenishment," 71.

9. *LETTERS: A Novel* (New York, 1982), 526–28; hereafter cited in the text.

10. Bellamy, *New Fiction*, 4.

11. Hofstadter, *Gödel*, 470–71.

12. Reilly, "Interview," 19, 15.

13. Ibid., 14–15.

14. Max F. Schulz, "Barth, *Letters*, and the Great Tradition," *Genre* 14 no. 1 (Spring 1981):107–8. Although most of them were arrived at independently, many of my remarks about *LETTERS* echo Schulz's analysis and assessment.

15. Reilly, "Interview," 19–20, 3, 14–15.

16. Schulz, "Barth," 98–99, 102.

17. Barth himself has stated that it is his "earnest hope" that "even the more fantastic characters—such as Bray, who might be a large insect of some kind—elicit a certain amount of sympathy by the novel's close." See Reilly, "Interview," 18–19.

18. The words quoted in this clause are from Schulz, "Barth," 104.

19. See Hofstadter, *Gödel*, 10.

20. In both his fiction and authorial statements, Barth has often indicated that he began *LETTERS* in the late 1960s, putting it aside to pursue *Chimera*, creating a separate work out of three tales he originally intended to incorporate in the novel. See, for example, Morrell, *John Barth*, 140–41 and the capsule "history" provided in *LETTERS* itself, 49.

21. *Sabbatical: A Romance* (New York, 1982), 14–15, 83–84; hereafter cited in the text.

22. In characterizing romance here and throughout the chapter I have drawn heavily upon Frye's summary; see especially *Anatomy*, 186–95.

23. See Reilly, "Interview," 22.

24. Frye, *Anatomy*, 36–37.

25. Ibid., 193, 201.

Chapter Nine

1. "Hawkes and Barth Talk about Fiction," *New York Times Book Review*, 1 April 1979, 32.

2. Jerome Mazzaro, *Postmodern American Poetry* (Urbana: University of Illinois Press, 1980), viii.

3. "The Literature of Replenishment," 69.

4. "Hawkes and Barth Talk About Fiction," 32.
5. "The Literature of Replenishment," 66.
6. Schulz, "Barth," 105.
7. Reilly, "Interview," 4.
8. Barth to E. P. Walkiewicz, 5 June 1985.
9. "The Literature of Replenishment," 69; Hofstadter, *Gödel*, 719.

Selected Bibliography

PRIMARY SOURCES

1. Books

Chimera. New York: Random House, 1972; paperback edition, New York: Fawcett Crest, 1973.

The End of the Road. Garden City, N.Y.: Doubleday & Co., 1958; rev. ed., Garden City, N.Y.: Doubleday & Co., 1967; paperback edition, New York: Bantam Books, 1981.

The Floating Opera. New York: Appleton-Century-Crofts, 1956; rev. ed., Garden City, N.Y.: Doubleday & Co., 1967; paperback edition, New York: Bantam Books, 1981.

Giles Goat-Boy; or, The Revised New Syllabus. Garden City, N.Y.: Doubleday & Co., 1966; paperback edition, New York: Bantam Books, 1981.

LETTERS: A Novel. New York: Putnam, 1979; paperback edition, New York: Fawcett Columbine, 1982.

Lost in the Funhouse: Fiction for Print, Tape, Live Voice. Garden City, N.Y.: Doubleday & Co., 1968; paperback edition, New York: Bantam Books, 1969.

Sabbatical: A Romance. New York: Putnam, 1982; paperback edition, New York: Putnam, 1982.

The Sot-Weed Factor. Garden City, N.Y.: Doubleday & Co., 1960; rev. ed., Garden City, N.Y.: Doubleday & Co., 1967; paperback edition, New York: Bantam Books, 1969.

2. Short Stories and Novellas

"Ambrose His Mark." *Esquire*, February 1963, 97, 122–27.

"Autobiography: A Self-Recorded Fiction." *New American Review* 2 (1968):72–75.

"Bellerophoniad." *Fiction* 1, no. 2 (1972):16–19. Excerpt.

"Dunyazadiad." *Esquire*, June 1972, 136–42, 158–68.

"Help! A Stereophonic Narrative for Authorial Voice." *Esquire*, September 1969, 108–9.

"Landscape: The Eastern Shore." *Kenyon Review* 22 (1960):104–10.

"Lilith and the Lion." *Hopkins Review* 4 (1950):49–53.

"Lost in the Funhouse." *Atlantic Monthly*, November 1967, 73–82.

"Night-Sea Journey." *Esquire*, June 1966, 82–83, 147–48.

"Perseid." *Harper's Magazine,* October 1972, 79–96.
"Petition." *Esquire,* July 1968, 68–71, 135.
"The Remobilization of Jacob Horner." *Esquire,* July 1958, 55–59.
"Test Borings." In *Modern Occasions,* edited by Philip Rahv, 247–63. New York: Farrar, Straus, & Giroux, 1966.
"Title." *Yale Review* 57 (1968):213–21.
"Water-Message." *Southwest Review* 48 (1963):226–37.

3. Nonfiction
Afterword to *The Adventures of Roderick Random,* by Tobias Smollett. New York: New American Library Signet Classics, 1964, 469–79.
"Censorship—1967: A Series of Symposia." *Arts in Society* 4 (1967):265–358.
"A Gift of Books." *Holiday,* December 1966, 171–72, 174, 177.
Letter to the Editor. *Dorchester News* (Cambridge, Md.), 9 August 1967, 2.
"The Literature of Exhaustion." *Atlantic Monthly,* August 1967, 29–34.
"The Literature of Replenishment: Postmodernist Fiction." *Atlantic,* January 1980, 65–71.
"Muse, Spare Me." *Book Week,* 26 September 1965, 28–29.
"My Two Muses." *Johns Hopkins Magazine,* April 1961, 9–13.
"*The Ocean of Story.*" In *Directions in Literary Criticism: Contemporary Approaches to Literature,* edited by Stanley Weintraub and Philip Young, 1–6. University Park: Pennsylvania State University Press, 1973.
Preface to "Lost in the Funhouse." In *Writer's Choice,* edited by Rust Hills, 1–2. New York: David McKay, 1974.
"A Tribute to John Hawkes." *Harvard Advocate,* October 1970, 11.
"A Tribute to Vladimir Nabokov." *TriQuarterly* 17 (Winter 1970):350. Also in *Nabokov: Criticism, Reminiscences, Translations and Tributes,* edited by Alfred Appel, Jr., and Charles Newman, 350. Evanston, Ill.: Northwestern University Press, 1970.

4. Interviews and Statements
Bellamy, Joe David. "Algebra and Fire: An Interview with John Barth." *Falcon* 4 (Spring 1972):5–15.
———. "Having It Both Ways: A Conversation Between John Barth and Joe David Bellamy." *New American Review* 15 (1972):134–50.
———. "John Barth." In *The New Fiction: Interviews with Innovative American Writers,* 1–18. Urbana: University of Illinois Press, 1974. Reprint of the previous entry.
Cooper, Arthur. "An In-Depth Interview with John Barth." *Harrisburg Patriot,* 30 March 1965, 6.
David, Douglas M. "The End Is a Beginning for Barth's 'Funhouse.' " *National Observer,* 16 September 1968, 19.

Enck, John J. "John Barth: An Interview." *Wisconsin Studies in Contemporary Literature* 6 (1965):3–14.

Golwyn, Judith. "New Creative Writers: 35 Novelists Whose First Work Appears This Season." *Library Journal* 81, no. 11 (1956):1496–97.

"Hawkes and Barth Talk About Fiction." *New York Times Book Review*, 1 April 1979, 7.

Henkle, Roger. "Symposium Highlights: Wrestling (American Style) with Proteus." *Novel* 3, no. 3 (1970):197–207.

"Heroic Comedy." *Newsweek*, 8 August 1966, 81–82.

"John Barth." In *First Person: Conversations on Writers and Writing*, edited by Frank Gado, 110–41. Schenectady, N.Y.: Union College Press, 1973.

McKenzie, James. "Pole-Vaulting in Top Hats: A Public Conversation with John Barth, William Gass, and Ishmael Reed." *Modern Fiction Studies* 22, no. 2 (1976):131–51.

Meras, Phyllis. "John Barth: A Truffle No Longer." *New York Times Book Review*, 7 August 1966, 22.

Prince, Alan. "An Interview with John Barth." *Prism* (Sir George Williams University), Spring 1968, 42–62.

Reilly, Charlie. "An Interview with John Barth." *Contemporary Literature* 22, no. 1 (1981):1–23.

"The Revolving Bookstand." *American Scholar* 34 (Summer 1965):474.

Shenker, Israel. "Complicated Simple Things." *New York Times Book Review*, 24 September 1972, 35–38.

5. Recordings

John Barth Reads from Giles Goat-Boy. New York: CMS Records, 1968, LP disc #551.

Novelist John Barth: Mythology Recycled for Today. North Hollywood, Calif.: Audio Text Cassettes, 1975, cassette #31810.

Prose Readings by John Barth. New York: McGraw-Hill, 1970, tape cassette #81575; reel to reel #75988.

Two Narratives for Tape and Live Voice. New York: McGraw-Hill, 1970, tape cassette #81673; reel to reel #78162.

SECONDARY SOURCES

1. Bibliographies

Vine, Richard Allan. *John Barth: An Annotated Bibliography.* Metuchen, N.J.: Scarecrow Press, 1977.

Walsh, Thomas P., and Northouse, Cameron. *John Barth, Jerzy Kosinski, and Thomas Pynchon: A Reference Guide.* Boston: G. K. Hall, 1977.

Weixlmann, Joseph. *John Barth: A Bibliography*. New York: Garland, 1976.

2. Books

Harris, Charles B. *Passionate Virtuosity: The Fiction of John Barth*. Urbana: University of Illinois Press, 1983. The most thorough scholarly study of Barth's oeuvre published to date, Harris's work is "an exercise in applied criticism" that examines Barth's first seven books in an effort to demonstrate that *LETTERS* constitutes the end of a stage in his development. Focusing on the idea of unity, Harris brings to bear the thought of Heidegger, Nietzsche, Campbell, Eliade, Jung, Lacan, Laing, and others. While the reader familiar with Barth's fiction will undoubtedly find it extremely intriguing and rewarding, it is not a book intended for the neophyte.

Joseph, Gerhard. *John Barth*. University of Minnesota Pamphlets on American Writers, no. 91. Minneapolis: University of Minnesota Press, 1970. A brief and early introduction covering Barth's work through *Lost in the Funhouse*.

Morrell, David. *John Barth: An Introduction*. University Park: Pennsylvania State University Press, 1976. Provides extremely useful background information about all the works through *Chimera*. Particularly helpful for those interested in biography, sources, and the process of composition.

Tharpe, Jac. *John Barth: The Comic Sublimity of Paradox*. Carbondale: Southern Illinois University Press, 1974. An excellent study covering the major works through *Chimera*. Tharpe's main focus is on the philosophical content of Barth's books, and he deals extensively with the author's interest in ethics, ontology, cosmology, epistemology, aesthetics, and logic.

Waldmeir, Joseph, ed. *Critical Essays on John Barth*. Boston: G. K. Hall, 1980. A fine collection of essays surveying Barth's work and the state of Barth criticism, and of reviews of and articles about each of his first six books. Contains a number of the best short critical studies produced so far.

3. Parts of Books

Allen, Mary. *The Necessary Blankness: Women in Major American Fiction of the Sixties*. Urbana: University of Illinois Press, 1976. Discusses Barth's depiction of women, praising his unusual ability to relate and relate to their condition.

Bryant, Jerry H. *The Open Decision: The Contemporary American Novel and Its Intellectual Background*. New York: Free Press, 1970. Dealing with Barth's first three novels, Bryant discusses the ethical dimension of his fiction and places his work in a context that includes many of his contemporaries.

Caramello, Charles. *Silverless Mirrors: Book, Self & Postmodern American Fiction*. Tallahassee: University Presses of Florida, 1983. The chapter on Barth and Eugene Wildman represents one of the most convincing attempts to read Barth's work in the context of contemporary critical theory. The book as a whole is one of the best studies of postmodern fiction available.

Harris, Charles B. *Contemporary American Novelists of the Absurd*. New Haven: College & University Press, 1971. The chapter on Barth serves as a helpful, if brief, introduction to his absurdist tendencies and his use of parody, imitation, and ultimacy.

Hauck, Richard Boyd. *A Cheerful Nihilism: Confidence and "The Absurd" in American Humorous Fiction*. Bloomington: Indiana University Press, 1971. Covering the novels from *The Floating Opera* to *Giles Goat-Boy*, and discussing at length "Night-Sea Journey" and "Lost in the Funhouse," Hauck, like Harris, argues that Barth is an absurdist and relates his treatment of values to his general aesthetic.

Karl, Frederick R. *American Fictions 1940–1980: A Comprehensive History and Critical Evaluation*. New York: Harper & Row, 1983. In a chapter on Pynchon and Barth, Karl reads the major works of the latter as informed by the effort to achieve "liberation from systematic control."

Kennard, Jean E. *Number and Nightmare: Forms of Fantasy in Contemporary Fiction*. Hamden, Conn.: Anchor, 1975. Explores the relationship between Barth's fiction and existentialist thought.

Klinkowitz, Jerome. *Literary Disruptions: The Making of a Post-Contemporary American Fiction*. Urbana: University of Illinois Press, 1975. Klinkowitz's vehemently negative appraisal of Barth's fiction is based on the unconvincing proposition that he, like Thomas Pynchon, is a "regressive parodist."

Kostelanetz, Richard. *The New American Arts*. New York: Horizon Press, 1965. Contains an early and fairly positive assessment of Barth's contribution to contemporary fiction. Kostelanetz's approach is more often impressionistic or descriptive rather than analytical.

Lehan, Richard. *A Dangerous Crossing: French Literary Existentialism and the Modern American Novel*. Carbondale: Southern Illinois University Press, 1973. Briefly analyzes Barth's first three books as well as "Night-Sea Journey," "Lost in the Funhouse," and "Life-Story," focusing on the self and values.

McConnell, Frank D. *Four Postwar American Novelists: Bellow, Mailer, Barth, and Pynchon*. Chicago: University of Chicago Press, 1977. Arguing that Barth's aim is to create a mythology in the face of contemporary dislocations and ultimacy, McConnell is at times overly discursive and makes little or no effort to acknowledge or respond to other readings of the fiction.

Olderman, Raymond M. *Beyond the Wasteland: A Study of The American Novel in the Nineteen Sixties.* New Haven: Yale University Press, 1972. Concentrating almost solely on *Giles Goat-Boy,* Olderman proposes that the book can be read as a response to Eliot's' poems, traces Barth's use of the work of Joseph Campbell and Lord Raglan, and suggests that he, like many other contemporary American novelists, draws on both the romance and the fable.

Scholes, Robert. *The Fabulators.* New York: Oxford University Press, 1967. Scholes's influential book compares Barth's fiction with that of Lawrence Durrell, Iris Murdoch, Kurt Vonnegut, Jr., Terry Southern, and John Hawkes. Viewing Barth as one of a group of modern writers who emphasize "art and joy," Scholes discusses the allegorical aspects of *Giles Goat-Boy.*

Schulz, Max F. *Black Humor Fiction of the Sixties: A Pluralistic Definition of Man and His World.* Athens: Ohio University Press, 1973. Extensively analyzing *Lost in the Funhouse* and discussing other of Barth's books as well, Schulz convincingly examines Barth's use of multiplicity and "Black Humor pluralism" as a response to contemporary limitations.

Stark, Jack O. *The Literature of Exhaustion: Borges, Nabokov, and Barth.* Durham, N.C.: Duke University Press, 1974. The long section on Barth includes a useful analysis of language and technique, but Stark occasionally goes overboard in attempting to link the fiction to "The Literature of Exhaustion."

Tanner, Tony. *City of Words: American Fiction 1950–1970.* New York: Harper & Row, 1971. The chapter on Barth in this excellent survey relates Wittgenstein's propositions about logic and language to Barth's propensity for verbal play.

Tilton, John W. *Cosmic Satire in the Contemporary Novel.* Lewisburg, Pa.: Bucknell University Press, 1977. Comparing *Giles Goat-Boy* with works by Anthony Burgess and Kurt Vonnegut, Jr., this brief book examines Barth's tragisatiric vision and use of myth as responses to the disintegration of the self.

Werner, Craig Hansen. *Paradoxical Resolutions: American Fiction since Joyce.* Urbana: University of Illinois Press, 1982. Contains a brief section on Barth that deals with "the writer as performer," concentrating mainly on *Giles* and *LETTERS.*

4. Articles

Diser, Philip E. "The Historical Ebenezer Cooke." *Critique* 10 (1968):48–59. An intriguing and useful comparison of *The Sot-Weed Factor* and Ebenezer Cooke's original poem; Barth's fictional biography and the historical novel.

Ewell, Barbara. "John Barth: The Artist of History." *Southern Literary Journal* 5 (1973):32–46. An important article that compares Burlingame's and Eben's approaches to the past, relates them to Barth's treatment of history in the book, and examines his attitudes toward art, imposed order, and enlightened innocence.

Farwell, Harold. "John Barth's Tenuous Affirmation: 'The Absurd, Unending Possibility of Love.' " *Georgia Review* 28 (1974):290–306. A survey of Barth's treatment of the subject from "Shirt of Nessus" to "Dunyazadiad" that pays particular attention to "Menelaiad."

Kiernan, Robert F. "John Barth's Artist in the Fun House." *Studies in Short Fiction* 10 (1973):373–80. An excellent examination of *Lost in the Funhouse* as *Künstlerroman*.

Kyle, Carol A. "The Unity of Anatomy: The Structure of Barth's *Lost in the Funhouse*." *Critique* 13 (1972):31–43. Employing Frye's definition of anatomy, Kyle moves through the stories in the series, comparing the book to such works as *Tristram Shandy* and *The Anatomy of Melancholy*, and addressing Barth's use of parody and contrapuntal composition.

LeClair, Thomas. "John Barth's *The Floating Opera*: Death and the Craft of Fiction." *Texas Studies in Literature and Language* 14 (1973):711–30. A perceptive analysis of Todd's roles as narrator and his use of his craft as a means of attempting to escape limitation and mortality.

Schulz, Max F. "Barth, *Letters*, and the Great Tradition." *Genre* 14 (1981):95–115. An excellent attempt to engage the novel in its entirety, Schulz's article deals with its biological ontology, its treatment of American history and culture, and its place in the literary tradition.

Smith, Herbert F. "Barth's Endless Road." *Critique* 6 (1963):68–76. Although much of what Smith says here has since been echoed by others, the article still serves as a helpful introduction to some of the basic subjects and techniques of *The End of the Road*, including ethics, existentialism, allegory, and the love-triangle.

Tatham, Campbell. "The Gilesian Monomyth: Some Remarks on The Structure of *Giles Goat-Boy*." *Genre* 3 (1970):364–75. Explores the similarities and differences between the pattern of Barth's book and those described by Campbell and Raglan, emphasizing that *Giles* deviates from such systems in its approaches to apotheosis and revelation.

Index